I0521098

Part of the Series—
Semillas de Luz

IS THERE ANYONE?

A CALL TO THOSE WHO WERE BORN FOR SOMETHING MORE

SAUL MIRANDA

© 2026 **Saul Miranda**

All rights reserved.

No part of this publication may be reproduced, stored in a retrieval system, or transmitted in any form or by any means—electronic, mechanical, photocopying, recording, or otherwise—without the prior written permission of the author, except for brief quotations used in reviews or critical articles.

Scripture quotations are taken from the **New King James Version**® (NKJV). © 1982 by Thomas Nelson.

Used by permission. All rights reserved.

First Edition: January 2026
ISBN: 979-8-9942363-1-4
Imprint: Editorial Semillas de Luz
Printed in the USA

Editing and Proofreading: Elizabeth Vargas
profa.vargas@gmail.com
Design and Layout: Saul Miranda
Published under the personal imprint: **Editorial Semillas de Luz**

Contact:
Saul Miranda
semillasdeluz2025@icloud.com

"Saul Miranda's writing style drew me in from the first line. The spiritual insights shared were incredibly deep, bringing new meaning to familiar Bible stories.

This book will be a great benefit to anyone who wonders if they've been disqualified from God's call for any reason. It will also encourage any Christian who longs for a deeper walk with God. I highly recommend this book and am so glad I read it."

— *Jenny Alexander, Readers' Favorite (5-Star Review)*

**EDITORIAL
SEMILLAS
DE LUZ**

First and foremost, to God, the source of my inspiration and purpose.

To Milka, my wife and best friend, thank you for walking with me through every season.

To my sons, Christian, Joel, and Jonathan — may you never forget that true direction is found only in God.

And to you, dear reader, because I am convinced that in every generation there will always be someone who says, **"Lord, here I am."**

My prayer is that, as you turn these pages, you will hear your own name in God's calling.

TABLE OF CONTENTS

PROLOGUE

"Search me, O God, and know my heart; try me, and know my anxieties; and see if there is any wicked way in me, and lead me in the way everlasting."

Psalm 139:23–24

David asks God to examine his life deeply—even his thoughts. It is like a spiritual exploratory surgery in which we are confronted by God with ourselves. Confrontation—a key word for me on this literary journey.

Facing the great responsibility of presenting this spiritual literary work before you makes me tremble and feel deeply honored. I call it a literary work because the metaphorical artistry employed by the author from beginning to end unmistakably leads the reader to recognize that only someone who truly knows the Word of God could express it so clearly and precisely, using a metaphorical language that penetrates the soul—even of those who may not yet know it.

Confrontation was the word that continually struck my mind throughout this literary journey, because I understand confrontation as the process of having a face-to-face encounter with the truth. The reading of each chapter presents questions asked by God—questions that were deeply unsettling to me—because they lead you into confrontation with yourself, with your inner being, which we often avoid examining because it frightens us, weakens us, and revives past or present wounds that have not yet healed and are in need of restoration.

Each chapter reminds us of God's faithfulness… but through different wounds.

Many times, I wept as I read, because I understood that God asks questions not to obtain information, but to transform us. God desires to touch us from within, to transform our inner being and our heart in the process of His divine surgery.

Above all, God spoke to me through this literary journey and confirmed that His questions become a calling to an imperfect being who needs to be shaken and transformed.

Who better than Saul Miranda Nieves to present this spiritual literary work? A man of God whom I have known since childhood. I have known him as a worshiper, musician, choir director, and teacher—but above all, as the husband of my daughter and an exemplary father.

He has been shaped through the process of living—through seasons in which he drifted away from his foundational principles—but in his renewed pursuit, he understood that the Person of the Holy Spirit came to form his character, shape his way of thinking, correct his way of loving, and align his decision-making. The Holy Spirit came to mature his character—and that process is painful.

He himself writes:

"I carry very visible scars," but I heard the voice of God saying to me, "Because your wounds do not disqualify My calling; they are the room where I will manifest Myself."

What 1 Corinthians 1:27–29 declares becomes a living reality:

"But God has chosen the foolish things of the world to put to shame the wise, and God has chosen the weak things of the world to put to shame the things which are mighty; and the base things of the world and the things which are despised God has chosen, and the things which are not, to bring to

nothing the things that are, that no flesh should glory in His presence."

I admire in Saul his unique and special ability to present biblical characters who, through confrontation and unsettling questions that alter the course of lives, are able to shake the soul, the spirit, and our entire internal structure.

If I were to summarize the message that I, as a reader, receive from this spiritual literary work, I would say this: every true calling requires a painful surrender. God is not looking for robots, but for those who obey His calling; and before sending you, God must shake your spiritual awakening, renew your mind, break old patterns, and lead you to embrace the mind of Christ.

Saul confronts us with our excuses before the imminent question: Is there anyone?

This book challenges us to respond, because God does not call spectators... He calls participants. He calls you. And this calling is activated with a single phrase:

"Here I am. Send me."

Remember... not another day. Not another season. Today.

"Also I heard the voice of the Lord, saying: 'Whom shall I send, And who will go for Us?' Then I said, 'Here am I! Send me.'"

Isaiah 6:8

Rev. Luz Amparo Melendez, NBCC
National Board Certified Counselor

PREFACE

Throughout my life, I have heard preachers raise their voices and ask:

"Is there anyone who will lift their hands in worship?"
"Is there anyone who will open their heart to receive what God has today?"

Those questions have their place—but there is one that pursues me with greater force.
It is not a light invitation to a momentary gesture.
It is an eternal, urgent, inescapable question.
It is the very voice of God piercing the heart:

Is there anyone?

- Is there anyone... willing to step beyond comfort?

- Is there anyone... ready to let go of excuses and embrace the calling?

- Is there anyone... bold enough to believe when everything around them cries the opposite?

Because the truth is this: we all have excuses.
Fear. Weariness. Comparison. Wounds. The past.
Excuses that seem reasonable, but eventually become invisible chains.

And there comes a moment when continuing to collect excuses is the same as surrendering purpose.

I have been there myself. I have asked in silence:

"Is there anyone who hears me?"
"Is there anyone who will reach out a hand?"
"Is there anyone who will forgive me after I fail?"

And I discovered that there was—
a present God, more real than my doubts, extending His hand at the exact moment.
That same God is the One calling you today.

He does not ask for perfection—only willingness.
He does not ask for elaborate answers—only a heart that says,
"Here I am."

This book is not a theological essay or a collection of beautiful phrases.
It is a holy confrontation.
Each chapter is a question God asks, and every question demands a response.

Because the voice of the Holy Spirit continues to resound—clear and direct:

Is there anyone who will stop hiding behind excuses?
Is there anyone who will no longer negotiate with fear?
Is there anyone who will rise in faith, even while trembling?

Is there anyone who will say, "Lord, I want to be that someone"?

I do not write to entertain you.
I write to awaken you.
So that when you close this book, you are left with no option but to kneel and respond to the God who is asking.

The question is in the air.
The answer is on your lips.

— Saul Miranda

THE THRESHOLD OF THE CALLING

There comes a moment in life when excuses lose their validity and silence is no longer comfortable. That moment arrives when God asks a question. It is not a casual curiosity, nor a passing interest. It is a voice that cuts through routine, pierces the heart, and demands a response.

From the very beginning, God has chosen to use questions to reveal what truly dwells within us. Not because He needs information—He knows all things—but because a question brings to the surface what we hide beneath layers of fear, insecurity, or pride.

A question from God does not seek data; it seeks awakening.

The entire Bible is a divine dialogue with humanity. Questions God asks ordinary men and women—questions that end up shaping history. Questions that transform a personal destiny, but also open a path for generations. Every inquiry from heaven carries an echo that travels through the centuries and still reaches us today: "Is there anyone…?"

This book is born from that echo. It is not an academic treatise nor an exhaustive theological commentary. It is, rather, an intimate journey—an open conversation between the voice of God and the response of the human heart. A walk through biblical moments where a single question changed everything: a shepherd who becomes a deliverer, a fearful fisherman who is transformed into a preacher, a persecutor who becomes an apostle.

And here is the truth: those questions were not trapped in antiquity. They are still alive. They still resound. They are still searching for an echo in each of us. Because the voice that questioned Moses, David, Peter, or Paul is the same voice that looks at you today and confronts you.

To enter these pages is to accept an invitation. It is to place yourself in the shoes of those who heard the voice of God and had to decide whether they would respond. It is to look at your hands, your thoughts, your fears—and hear heaven whisper your name with a direct question.

This is not a comfortable reading. It will be like a mirror that reveals, like a fire that purifies, like a whispering breeze. But it is also a journey filled with hope, because every divine question does not end in condemnation, but in purpose.

You are standing at the threshold. Before the first question. Before the chapters of this eternal dialogue unfold.

The decision is yours:

Will you continue reading as a curious spectator, or as someone who already senses the voice calling?

Because when you turn the page, you will not only enter the story of Abraham.

You will enter your own story.

CHAPTER 1

WOULD YOU GIVE ME WHAT YOU LOVE MOST?

TRUST THE ETERNAL, BUT SURRENDER THE IMMEDIATE

ABRAHAM

A DIFFERENT CALL FROM ROUTINE

We often imagine God's callings as something "big." We think of figures who make headlines or leaders who move crowds. We picture Moses lifting a staff that parts seas, or politicians and governors signing laws. Yet in the eyes of the Creator, it is not the size of the platform that defines the magnitude of a calling, but the obedience with which we respond. Every invitation from God—from the simplest to the most visible—is an opportunity to experience His character and His provision.

And there is a key detail: many times God calls us without giving us a map. His voice says, "Go," without including all the coordinates. He tells us, "Do it," without providing a budget. This is not an administrative oversight of heaven; it is an intentional design. The more we trust Him, the less we depend on details in order to obey.

God leads us through points of faith, not detailed maps.

AN ORDINARY MAN
WITH AN EXTRAORDINARY CALLING

In this story appears Abraham—a name that resonates as the "father of faith" and as the man who fathered a son at one hundred years of age. But before becoming a patriarch, Abraham was Abram—a man of flesh and blood, with doubts and fears. His name, Abram, meant "exalted father," but God would change his name to Abraham, "father of a multitude." This name change was not spiritual marketing; it was the reflection of a divine promise. And although today we revere him as a hero, in his time he had to learn to trust a God who spoke to him in a radically new way.

To set the scene: Abram was born in Ur of the Chaldeans, a prosperous city in ancient Mesopotamia. His father, Terah, set out with his family toward Canaan, but they stopped in Haran and settled there. In that place, God spoke to Abram with words as concise as they were unsettling:

> *"Get out of your country, from your family and from your father's house, to a land that I will show you".*
>
> (Genesis 12:1)

In other words: pack your bags and start walking; the destination will be revealed along the way. Who undertakes a journey like that?

He left Haran with his wife Sarai and all his possessions. Commentators estimate that from Ur to Canaan is nearly 1,500 kilometers (about 930 miles). To put that into perspective, it would be like walking today from Orlando to Philadelphia. And take note—no GPS, no rest stops, no Chick-fil-A along the way to grab a meal. In ancient times, traveling that distance was a journey that could take months, not days. Every mile was an opportunity to turn back and reconsider. Yet Abram kept going. Why? Because the voice he heard did not ask him to prove his faith; it offered him a covenant of trust.

BLIND TRUST:
THE FIRST STEP WITHOUT DETAILS

Biblical faith does not begin with clarity; it begins with obedience. In Genesis 12, we see that God did not offer Abraham an itinerary in advance. He simply promised to make him a great nation, to bless him, and to make him a blessing to others. He promised him a name, a place, and a purpose.

Abraham did not know the names of the cities he would pass through. He did not carry a list of hosts who would receive him along the way. What he had was a promise, a calling, and—above all—a relationship with a God who was new and different from the gods of his culture.

He responded with radical trust: he went out not knowing where he was going, and without negotiating every step along the way.

WHEN THE PROMISE FEELS SLOW: ISAAC AND GOD'S TIMING

The years passed. Abraham obeyed, yet he did not see the tangible fulfillment of the promise. God had promised that he would become the father of many nations, but his wife Sarai was barren, and time kept moving forward.

At seventy-five years old, Abraham obeyed and set out, just as Scripture says:

> *"Abram was seventy-five years old when he departed from Haran"*.
>
> *(Genesis 12:4)*

But he received the promised son at one hundred years old:

Genesis 21:5

In other words, he waited a quarter of a century. And what do you do during twenty-five years of waiting? How do you sustain faith when calendars stretch on and wrinkles begin to appear?

When Abraham and Sarah moved ahead of God's plan, Ishmael was born. God, in His mercy, did not reject him, but promised Hagar:

> "Yet I will also make a nation of the son of the bondwoman, because he is your seed".
>
> (Genesis 21:13)

And that nation grew and multiplied, becoming the origin of many Arab peoples. While Isaac was the son of the promise, Ishmael was also blessed—but the conflict between them began in a tent thousands of years ago and can still be seen reflected in the Middle East today. Two brothers, two lineages, two peoples who share blood and, at the same time, carry deep historical tensions.

Even today, when we hear news of wars, divisions, or disputes over sacred land, we are witnessing the echoes of that human decision to move ahead of what God had promised. The promise was not canceled—Isaac remained the son of the covenant—but a chain of conflicts was set in motion, conflicts that still wound the world. It all began with the impatience of a man and a woman who thought they could "help" God.

The lesson is clear and practical for you and for me: when we try to force the promise, we create Ishmaels. Ishmaels that we later grieve over, that bring division within families, that create tension in the church or in our personal lives. It is not that God fails to keep His word; it is that our shortcuts add battles that were never part of His original design. The cost of impatience is not always paid only by the one who decides—often it is paid by the generations that follow.

PROMISE FULFILLED AND TRUST RENEWED: THE ARRIVAL OF ISAAC

Despite the impatience of Abraham and Sarah, God remained faithful. Genesis 21 describes the miracle:

> *"And the LORD visited Sarah as He had said, and the LORD did for Sarah as He had spoken. For Sarah conceived and bore Abraham a son in his old age".*
>
> *(Genesis 21:1–2)*

This was the long-awaited Isaac, whose name means "laughter." Why? Because when God announced that they would have a son, Sarah laughed in disbelief *(Genesis 18:12)*. And years later, that promise produced a different kind of laughter—the joy of seeing the impossible become reality.

Isaac was not just a baby; he was the tangible link to the promise. In him rested the future of the nation God would raise up. Each morning, as Abraham awoke and saw Isaac, he was reminded of the faithfulness of a God who does not lie.

THE GREATEST CHALLENGE: GIVE WHAT YOU LOVE MOST

This was not the first time Abraham had given up a son. Years earlier, he had watched Ishmael, the son born of his impatience, depart when God asked him to let him go. For that reason, when God now asks for Isaac, Abraham is not only facing a difficult command, but the weight of a story that begins to ache all over again.

One might assume the story should end with a happy conclusion: promise fulfilled! But God still had something deeper to reveal to Abraham—something that goes beyond receiving promises: **the value of surrender.**

In Genesis 22, God tests Abraham in an extraordinary way. He asks him to offer Isaac as a sacrifice. To our modern eyes, this sounds brutal and incomprehensible. Yet in Abraham's time, sacrifices were common among pagan cultures. What is radical here is that the very God who abhors human sacrifice is asking His servant to do something that seems to collide head-on with the promise. How can the God who promises life ask for the death of the promised son?

Let us not forget a crucial detail: God is speaking to a man who is still learning to recognize the voice of the one true God. There is no Bible on Abraham's table. There is no catalog of sermons on YouTube. All Abraham has is a relationship built on what he has heard and experienced. His faith is grounded in encounters, not in a manual.

And it is within that relationship that God chooses to test his heart:

Will you obey when the request threatens your own security and your understanding?

THE SCENE AT MORIAH: OBEDIENCE IN THE TENSION

Mount Moriah is the setting. Abraham rises early, prepares the wood, and sets out on the journey with his son and two servants. For three days they walk, until they see from afar the hill to which God had led him. What conversations must have taken place along that road? How did Abraham conceal the tension within him?

Isaac—young and perceptive—notices the troubling absence of a lamb. He carries the wood on his shoulders—a detail that anticipates Jesus bearing His cross—and asks,

> "My father... Look, the fire and the wood, but where is the lamb for a burnt offering?"
>
> (Genesis 22:7)

Abraham's response is brief and powerful:

> "My son, God will provide for Himself the lamb for a burnt offering".
>
> (Genesis 22:8)

In other words: I do not have the details. I do not see the lamb. But I trust that God—the One who called me, promised me, and fulfilled His word—will provide.

They arrive. They build an altar. They arrange the wood. Abraham binds Isaac. The scene becomes unbearably tense: a father raising a knife over his beloved son—not because he does not love him, but precisely because he does.

And just as the knife is lifted high, a voice from heaven breaks the silence:

> "Abraham, Abraham! ... Do not lay your hand on the lad, nor do anything to him".
>
> (Genesis 22:11–12)

At that moment, Abraham lifts his eyes and sees a ram caught in a thicket. He offers it in place of Isaac. And on that altar, Abraham calls the place **Jehovah Jireh** — *"The LORD will provide"*—not because God finally gave him something he deserved, but because God revealed that His provision is found in the place of obedience.

TRUST THE ETERNAL, SURRENDER THE IMMEDIATE

What does it mean to trust the eternal and surrender the immediate? It means that in our daily lives, there will be moments when God asks us to pause or to let go of something we deeply value—not necessarily forever, but long enough to reveal whether our hearts are more rooted in that thing than in Him.

These "altars" may be relationships, dreams, habits, positions, or even hobbies. There are seasons when God asks us to release something that, although not sinful in itself, has become an idol—a place of affection that competes with our love for God.

Our world is filled with **immediacy.** Everything is "on demand": purchases with a click, food at the door in thirty minutes, streaming without commercials. And without realizing it, we transfer that mindset into our relationship with God. We want promises with push notifications. We expect His plan to adjust to our calendar. When the waiting stretches on, we begin to doubt His goodness.

But Abraham's life reminds us that faith embraces the eternal. It trusts the Word of God above the timeline.

Surrender the immediate: recognize that some things must die in order for the promise to flourish.

MY OWN "MORIAH" IN EVERYDAY LIFE

I grew up in the gospel, but it was not until I was nineteen years old that I consciously surrendered my life to Christ. From that moment on, my daily prayer sounded the same:

"Lord, make me new again. Holy Spirit, take control."

And I quickly learned that when the Holy Spirit takes that prayer seriously, He begins to point out very specific things that need to be surrendered.

First, it was friendships that pulled me away from God. Then, habits that held me captive. But the hardest thing of all was not letting go of what was wrong—it was letting go of what I loved: **movies.**

Cinema was not just a hobby; it was my passion. I could go to the movies two or three times a week. I even skipped college classes just to make the 11:15 a.m. showing. At home, I had my own personal museum of VHS tapes and DVDs, perfectly organized. Movies were my refuge—my private altar of red seats and popcorn.

One day, during prayer, God spoke to my heart:

"That thing you love so much… I want you to surrender it."

And I confess, I argued with Him.

"Lord, but it's not bad. I'm not hurting anyone. It's not a sin."

But I understood something then that I still hold onto today:

God does not always ask you for what is bad, but for what has become more important than Him in your life.

I obeyed. I stopped going to the movies. I packed away my collection. I spent one or two full years without setting foot in a theater. And remember—this was before Netflix and Disney+. This was the era of Blockbuster. I was a VIP customer. The employee greeted me by name. I am convinced that when I stopped showing up, they held an emergency meeting:

"What are we going to do without Saul? We just lost fifty percent of our profits."

What surprised me was what came next. What seemed like a loss, God transformed into purpose. The time I once dedicated to movies, He filled with opportunities: leading youth, teaching Sunday School, directing choirs, writing dramas, preaching, participating in street evangelism services, going on mission trips, and studying at Bible institute. God was not punishing me—He was preparing me. That sacrifice was, in reality, an investment.

And in the middle of all this—while I was "fasting from movies"—God was writing another story in parallel. I already knew Milka. She was a friend of my sister, and I was a friend of her brothers. We had crossed paths many times, but always in parallel lanes. And although at that time I did not yet feel the famous thump-thump in my heart, I already saw something different in her: her spiritual beauty.

Today, I understand God's move much better. He asked me to let go of an idol of entertainment, and in return He gave me an eternal gift. I traded movie theater seats for a stable home. I stored away my VHS collection and received the companionship of the woman He had prepared for me. I left Blockbuster, and God enrolled me in a lifetime plan—Milka included, with no expiration date.

What seemed like sacrifice was, in truth, the beginning of a life focused on purpose. I learned that when you obey and surrender the immediate, you discover that the eternal is always infinitely greater.

THE UNEXPECTED CALL: A RECENT LESSON ON GOD'S TIMING

I want to share a recent story that deeply impacted me and illustrates how God works according to **His** calendar, not ours. Not long ago, I was listening to a sermon by Pastor **Steven Furtick,** in which he spoke about Abraham and the principle of "let it go" in relation to promise and sacrifice. He explained how we often want God's promises to be fulfilled on our timeline, while God operates on His own.

As I listened intently to that message, my phone rang with a **FaceTime** call. It was **Jean Carlos**, my nephew-in-law (my wife Milka's nephew). It was unusual for him to call me on video, so I answered.

Jean Carlos was emotional—on the verge of tears. He said, "Uncle, remember that Jonathan—my youngest son—traveled to Tampa for an **Elevation Rhythm** concert." (If you're not familiar, Elevation Rhythm is the youth worship collective of **Elevation Church**, Pastor Furtick's church.) After the concert, they offered the opportunity to be baptized immediately. Jonathan hesitated because he wanted us to be present for such a special moment. But after praying, he decided to do it. Jean Carlos called so that Milka and I could witness it live through the phone.

We connected and saw Jonathan standing in the baptismal pool, a mixture of nerves and joy on his face. We watched him go down into the water and come back up in tears. It was a sacred moment. It wasn't on our calendar or in our church. It happened at the time and place God chose. His wet smile and his embrace with his girlfriend testified to an eternal decision.

After the baptism, Jonathan told us how meaningful the moment was for him and how this step confirmed his faith. Milka cried and laughed at the same time; I had a lump in my throat. We didn't plan that baptism—but God orchestrated it in His time.

That day, we were reminded once again: we cannot schedule God's work in the lives of our children. We can pray, guide, and walk alongside them, but **the direction of the journey belongs to the Lord.** Jonathan chose to be baptized because God called him in that moment—not before and not after. Had he been baptized out of our pressure, it might not have carried the same weight.

That improvised FaceTime call became an altar of gratitude. All we could do was rejoice and remember that God provides perfect moments, even when they are not on our agenda.

And once again, we understood this truth: God's clock is never late—it arrives exactly on time for a heart that is ready.

LEARNING TO WAIT AND LET GO: THE DIVINE CALENDAR

This lesson connects directly with Abraham: he waited twenty-five years for Isaac. We, too, wait years for the conversion or spiritual growth of someone we love. We grow impatient, but God does not operate on our schedule. He neither delays nor rushes—He arrives on time.

So what do we do? Sometimes the only thing we can do is tune ourselves to God's plan. We may not know the exact route, but we trust the One who leads the way. We surrender control. And as we walk, opportunities emerge—opportunities that only faith can see.

There are moments when God invites us to remain still:

"The LORD will fight for you, and you shall hold your peace".

(Exodus 14:14)

And there are other moments when He urges us to move forward:

"Why do you cry to Me? Tell the children of Israel to go forward".

(Exodus 14:15)

Both movements require faith. Waiting is not inactivity; it is active expectation. We must remember that some promises are fulfilled quickly, while others seem to take much longer. Hebrews 11 tells us that many died without receiving what was promised, yet they greeted it from afar. Faith transcends our calendars and fixes our eyes on eternity.

Even if we do not see everything now, we trust that God's story does not end with our tears or our disappointments.

FAITH THAT DOES NOT NEGOTIATE DETAILS

Let us return to the scene at Moriah and reflect on our own lives. What does it mean today to obey without negotiating details? Sometimes God asks us to abandon habits that bring us pleasure but draw us away from His presence. At other times, He calls us to give generously when the calculator screams, "There's no budget." He may ask us to release a relationship that has become an idol, or to let go of a professional dream that no longer aligns with His purpose.

Our response often mirrors Isaac's question:
"My father, here are the fire and the wood, but where is the lamb?"
And God responds:
"I will provide.
Put down the knife; trust Me."

This kind of faith is not irrational—it is trusting. Abraham was not a heartless robot; he was a father deeply in love with his son. But he understood that God was not asking for Isaac's life because He needed his body; He was asking for Abraham's heart. The ram in the thicket—Jehovah Jireh—appears when the heart is willing to obey.

When we trust, we do not demand explanations; when we distrust, we ask for every detail. The same dynamic exists with our teenage children. If we trust them, it is enough to say, "Be home by this time." But if trust is fragile, we multiply questions, require live location, and ask for photos. The less we trust, the more data we demand.

With God, it works the same way. Mature faith is not obsessed with the route, but with the Guide. It says, "Lord, I don't need the entire itinerary—I need Your presence." True faith is like a child who, after receiving permission, does not ask twenty times, "What if...?" but trusts that the Father's instruction is enough.

As we mature in Christ, we learn to live this way: less obsessed with details, more focused on His voice.

A MIRROR OF FAITH

Hebrews 11 is known as the "Hall of Faith." There, Abraham is mentioned alongside other heroes as an example of radical trust. The letter declares:

> *"By faith Abraham obeyed when he was called to go out to the place which he would receive as an inheritance. And he went out, not knowing where he was going".*
>
> *(Hebrews 11:8)*

And also:

> *"By faith Abraham, when he was tested, offered up Isaac".*
> *(Hebrews 11:17)*

The writer of Hebrews highlights that Abraham acted this way because he was "accounting that God was able to raise him up, even from the dead" *(Hebrews 11:19)*. He understood that if God had promised that his descendants would come through Isaac, then—even if Isaac were offered as a sacrifice—God would raise him up if necessary.

This is the kind of faith that trusts the eternal. It believes that God's promises have the final word, even over death itself.

WAITING IS NOT WASTING TIME: PATIENCE AS AN ACT OF FAITH

Abraham's waiting teaches us that patience is not passivity. Waiting twenty-five years did not mean watching television and counting days. It meant building altars, shepherding flocks, traveling through unknown lands, dealing with conflict, and listening to God. Patience is an act of faith because it is rooted in trust in the character of God.

Scripture tells us:

> "Knowing that the testing of your faith produces patience. But let patience have its perfect work, that you may be perfect and complete, lacking nothing".
>
> (James 1:3–4)

Waiting is a laboratory where God refines our faith. When we try to control the divine calendar, we reveal how fragile our trust can be. God, instead, invites us to remember that **He is the Author of time.**

WHAT IS YOUR ISAAC?

Although we do not live in Abraham's time nor hear the same command, God's tests are still very real. Our "Isaac" may be a professional dream, a romantic relationship, a life plan, or a hobby that has taken ownership of our passion. This is not about God taking pleasure in asking us for uncomfortable things. It is about a Father who knows that if we are not willing to let go, we will never experience the fullness of His provision.

If Abraham had clung to Isaac and refused to obey, Isaac

would have lived—but Abraham would never have known **Jehovah Jireh.** He would have remained trapped at a level of faith that never experienced God's greatest provision.

That is why it is worth asking ourselves: What in my life competes with God for my time, my thoughts, and my resources? What is God asking me to release in order to trust the eternal? It will not always be something sinful. Sometimes it is something good that has become too important.

When we try to "help" God, we do not cancel the promise— but we complicate the journey. In your case, it might be social media, video games, a toxic relationship, a professional dream, or even your own reputation.

AN INVITATION TO TRUST LIKE ABRAHAM

We have walked through Abraham's story and paused at his calling, his waiting, his mistakes, the promise of Isaac, and the test at **Moriah.** What remains?

It is not about being perfect—Abraham was not. It is about responding to God's invitation with trusting obedience. Someone might say, "I could never do what Abraham did." And you may be right—God is not asking you to sacrifice a son. But He is calling you to an act of faith that, for you, feels just as radical.

Do not focus on the greatness of the sacrifice; focus on the greatness of the promise.

Do not fix your eyes on the knife; fix them on the voice that says, **"I will provide for you."**

AN ALTAR IN OUR TIME

In the end, Abraham's story leaves us with questions and challenges. What altar are we willing to build in our own lives? To what extent do we trust that God has a ram for every act of obedience? Are we willing to be known for our faith rather than for our achievements?

Life is a series of altars: the altar of calling, the altar of waiting, the altar of failure, the altar of fulfilled promise, and the altar of surrender. Each altar is an encounter with the God who calls us to surrender the immediate in order to embrace the eternal.

If you find yourself in a season of waiting, remember that God is not standing still. He is working in silence. If you are tempted to take shortcuts, remember Ishmael and the tensions that followed. If God asks you for a sacrifice, remember that there is a ram you will only see when you climb the mountain. And if you feel unable to let go of what you love, look to **Jesus.**

He gave His life—the most precious gift—so that you and I might be called children of God. His sacrifice on the cross is the ultimate proof that God provides. In Christ, we have received a promise greater than Isaac, a new name greater than Abraham's, and a hope that transcends our tears.

If today you are waiting, God is not inactive.

If today shortcuts tempt you, remember that they come at a cost.

If today He asks you for something valuable, look toward the thicket—the provision is waiting for you in the place of obedience.

PRAY LIKE THIS (OUT LOUD, IF YOU CAN)

Lord, I choose Your presence over my plans.

I entrust to You what I love most;
it does not belong to me—it is Yours.

Give me steady steps when I have no roadmap.

Teach me to trust Your process
when I do not understand the purpose.

Thank You, Jehovah Jireh;
on Your mountain, there is always provision. Amen.

This prayer is a starting point. The rest, as **Hebrews 12:2** reminds us, will depend on our willingness to "fix our eyes on Jesus, the author and finisher of our faith." He began this work in you, and He will complete it. Your role is to trust. His role is to provide.

Trust the eternal. Surrender the immediate…
and prepare to see the provision on the mountain—on your own **Moriah.**

In the end, the one who trusts does not need the map;
they need the **Guide.**

Climb the mountain holding what you love;
come down with a freer heart and a living faith.

CHAPTER 2

WILL YOU FORGIVE?

WITHIN EVERY WOUND THERE IS A DECISION THAT CHANGES DESTINIES

JOSEPH

"But Joseph said to them, 'Do not be afraid, for am I in the place of God?

But as for you, you meant evil against me; but God meant it for good, in order to bring it about as it is this day, to save many people alive.'"

(Genesis 50:19–20)

It is not the attack that defines your destiny, but what you do after the attack. Betrayal hurts, but more dangerous than the wound is the poison that can remain inside. The enemy does not win when he wounds you; he wins when he makes you bitter.

DREAMS AND A TUNIC — THE UNEXPECTED WOUND

Joseph was still an adolescent when God gave him dreams that did not fit within his home or his time. In one dream, he saw his brothers bowing down to his sheaf; in another, he saw the sun, the moon, and the stars bowing before him.

His father Jacob also gave him a tunic of many colors—as if divine favor needed a uniform. It was a gesture of love from a father to his favored son, but in a family where jealousy and rivalry were already at a breaking point, that tunic became fuel on a fire. His brothers felt displaced. At their table, plans of death began to simmer.

Joseph did not seek to be hated; he was hated for being blessed. The wound came without him provoking it.

Here lies the first decision: Joseph could have been consumed either by the pain of being misunderstood or by the pride of feeling special. Instead, he guarded God's dreams and honored his father's authority. He did not pursue fame; he pursued obedience. His identity was not found in the color of his tunic, but in the word of God. That decision allowed him to survive the day the tunic was torn from him and shredded to pieces.

Perhaps your "tunic" is a gift, an opportunity, or a favor that others do not understand. Perhaps you have been wounded for being different or for sharing your vision. You cannot prevent the envy of others from tearing your garment, but you can decide that your identity is not found in what you wear.

Forgiveness begins when you choose not to live defensively. You do not need to apologize for being blessed; you need to steward favor with humility. Forgiveness does not always begin with acknowledging guilt, but with acknowledging a wound. Joseph did not need to ask forgiveness for the dreams God gave him or for the favor he received—but he did have to carry the pain those dreams awakened in others.

Sometimes, even when we have done nothing wrong, love moves us to seek reconciliation with those who felt displaced, wounded, or confused. Forgiveness matures when we stop asking who was right and start asking how to heal what was broken. It is not about denying the blessing, but about stewarding favor with humility and with a heart willing to restore.

THE PIT—THE FIRST CROSSROAD

The brothers' plans moved from whispers to action. One day, while tending the flocks, they saw Joseph approaching from a distance and conspired to kill him. Reuben managed to keep them from shedding his blood; instead, they stripped him of his tunic and threw him into a dry pit. Later, when Reuben stepped away, Judah suggested selling him to a group of Ishmaelite merchants passing by. For **twenty pieces of silver,** they handed their brother over to a caravan bound for Egypt.

There, in the darkness of a pit that smelled of damp earth and abandonment, Joseph had to decide what to do with his pain. He could fill his heart with hatred and plan revenge, or he could place his life in God's hands. He chose the latter. Scripture does not record his thoughts, but the story proves the outcome: he did not allow bitterness to become his identity. Instead of shouting curses, he remained silent. Instead of swearing revenge, he chose trust.

We all have pits. A diagnosis, a betrayal, a financial collapse, a farewell, a secret we were thrown into without warning. The pit is not the end—but it can become a grave if bitterness buries you. The question is not whether you will fall into a pit, but how you will come out of the one you are already in. You can grow bitter over what was done to you, or you can decide that no one has the power to stop God's plan.

Forgiveness begins when you recognize that your heart is more valuable than any tunic that was taken from you.

POTIPHAR'S HOUSE— INTEGRITY UNDER PRESSURE

The merchants took Joseph to Egypt and sold him to Potiphar, captain of Pharaoh's guard. Joseph was a slave without rights, but his character did not need a title to stand out. Before long, Potiphar noticed that everything Joseph touched prospered, so he placed him in charge of his household. Joseph managed faithfully. His promotion within slavery was the reward of someone who knew how to serve.

Then another test arrived: Potiphar's wife set her eyes on him. Day after day, she invited him to her bed. For Joseph, it would have been easy to justify an affair—no one was watching, no one would find out, "surely there must be something good in all this." Instead, he answered with one of the most radical statements in Scripture:

> *"How then can I do this great wickedness, and sin against God?"*
>
> *(Genesis 39:9)*

The decision was clear: lose his position rather than lose his integrity. She, filled with resentment, accused him of attempted assault, and Potiphar imprisoned him without a trial.

The decision: Joseph chose to obey God without witnesses rather than gratify his flesh without immediate consequences. Forgiveness and faithfulness walk hand in hand. A heart that refuses to be seduced by bitterness is less likely to be seduced by temptation. His heart was governed by God, not by circumstances.

When life wounds you, the temptation to escape through forbidden pleasure grows stronger. You may think, "They owe me," "It's worth sinning," "No one will know." But integrity is a decision you make when the lights are off.

Forgiveness is also tested in those rooms where no one sees you—in how you speak about the one who hurt you, in how you treat the one who wounded you, in how you steward your pain.

Being faithful in what is small and hidden prepares you to steward what is great and public.

THE PRISON — FAITHFUL IN THE DARK

Innocent, yet imprisoned, Joseph was thrown into the prison beneath Potiphar's house. There were no colorful tunics or positions of trust there. Still, his character did not depend on a stage. Before long, the keeper of the prison entrusted him with the care of the other prisoners. Joseph served them and listened to them. His faithfulness did not depend on an audience.

In prison, he met two men—the cupbearer and the baker of Pharaoh—who had been sent there for an unknown offense. Both had troubling dreams. Joseph listened carefully and, by God's revelation, interpreted their dreams. To the cupbearer he announced restoration to his position; to the baker, execution. And so it happened. Joseph asked the cupbearer to remember him when he was restored—but the man forgot him completely. Two more years passed in the shadows.

The decision: in the darkness, Joseph kept serving. He did not grow silent out of resentment. He did not stop interpreting the dreams of others because his own dreams were on pause. His faithfulness in small things planted the seed of his deliverance. When Pharaoh had a dream no one could interpret, the cupbearer remembered the Hebrew in prison and spoke his name.

Sometimes the pit lasts for years. Injustice seems to stretch on, and the memory of what was done to you hurts even more when it is mixed with the silence of others. Forgiveness is cultivated in these cells. Every time you choose to speak well when you could speak ill, every time you choose to serve when you could sink into self-pity, you are interpreting dreams that are not your own. And one day—when you least expect it—someone will remember your name.

The door that opens suddenly is supported by yesterday's silent obedience.

THE PALACE—STEWARDSHIP OF FAVOR

When Pharaoh dreamed of thin cows devouring fat cows and withered heads of grain consuming full ones, no one in Egypt could interpret the message. That was when the cupbearer spoke of Joseph. He was taken out of prison, shaved, changed, and brought before the throne. Joseph listened to the dream and, with humility, said:

"It is not in me; God will give Pharaoh an answer of peace".

(Genesis 41:16)

He explained that seven years of abundance would be followed by seven years of famine. He proposed a plan of collection and wise administration to save the land from starvation. Pharaoh, impressed, appointed him governor of Egypt, second only to himself. He gave him a signet ring, an Egyptian name, and a wife. Joseph was not promoted by Potiphar, nor by the cupbearer, nor by Pharaoh—God promoted him because of his character.

The decision: Joseph did not use his position to take revenge or to show off. He used his power to preserve lives. The greatest temptation of forgiveness is not only found in pain; it appears when you finally have the chance to settle accounts. Joseph chose to govern with grace, not resentment. He managed Egypt's resources wisely and opened the storehouses to feed not only the nation, but the surrounding peoples as well.

Sometimes the test is not pain, but favor. When the opportunity comes to administer justice your way, remember that you are a steward, not an owner. Forgiveness is revealed in how you use your influence. Will it be to humiliate those who humiliated you—or to give them bread? Will it be to parade your ring—or to extend the table?

God's favor is not meant to be displayed like a tunic, but to be served out—like Joseph did.

THE REUNION — GRACE OVER THE OFFENSE

The famine struck the land, and Jacob sent his sons to Egypt to buy grain. Joseph, dressed as an Egyptian, recognized them immediately. They did not recognize him. He accused them of being spies and kept Simeon as a hostage. He demanded that they bring Benjamin to prove their honesty. It was a test—to see whether they were still the same men who had sold him.

When they returned with Benjamin, Joseph prepared a banquet for them, wept in secret, and then tested them once more by hiding his cup in Benjamin's sack. When it was found, he threatened to take Benjamin as a slave. At that moment, Judah offered himself in Benjamin's place. That act of sacrifice broke the wall.

Joseph could no longer restrain himself. He withdrew to weep, then returned and cried out,

"I am Joseph!" (Genesis 45:3

In that moment, the past and the present embraced. His brothers trembled, certain they would die. But Joseph drew near, kissed them, and said,

"You meant evil against me; but God meant it for good".
(Genesis 50:20)

He explained that everything he had endured was meant to preserve their lives. He invited them to bring their father and the entire family to Egypt. He gave them land in **Goshen** and cared for them. He did not harbor resentment; he used his power to provide them shelter and bread. After their father died, the brothers feared once again, but Joseph reaffirmed his forgiveness and promised to care for them.

The decision: Joseph transformed debt into provision. He did not deny the betrayal; he interpreted it through the lens of divine purpose. His forgiveness did not erase the past—it changed its meaning. He took the wound and turned it into a bridge.

At some point, the one who wounded you may return to your life. You will be standing in the palace of your calling and remembering the pit of your pain. Then you will decide: will you cast them out, or will you invite them to your table? Forgiveness is not naïve—it is courageous. It asks for proof, observes fruit, and sets boundaries. But when it sees repentance, it dares to embrace.

Because forgiveness transforms victims into channels: your life can feed others—even those who once wounded you.

FORGIVENESS DOES NOT ERASE THE PAST; IT REDEEMS IT

When Joseph said, "God meant it for good," he was not justifying his brothers' sin, nor the lie of Potiphar's wife, nor the cupbearer's forgetfulness. He named each wrong—but he placed it in God's hands. That is forgiveness: not pretending it doesn't hurt, but allowing God to change the purpose of that pain. The scar remains, but it is no longer a reminder of failure; it becomes a testimony of grace.

The cross is the greatest example: the death of the innocent became the salvation of the guilty. What the devil planned for destruction, God used to redeem the world. In the same way, your broken story can become the score of a miracle—if you choose to surrender it.

Saying "to forgive is to forget" is a dangerous myth. You do not need to erase memory in order to heal; you need to reinterpret it. You do not need to call evil good; you need to acknowledge the wrong and trust in God's justice. You do not need to keep walking with the one who wounded you if there is no fruit of repentance or change; you need to be free from resentment in order to rest. Forgiveness does not force immediate restoration; it leaves the door open for when repentance, boundaries, and wisdom are present.

Forgiving does not mean you will never feel pain again; it means you have decided not to feed that pain.

FORGIVENESS AS INNER GOVERNANCE

Jesus taught:

> *"Love your enemies, bless those who curse you, do good to those who hate you, and pray for those who mistreat you and persecute you".*
>
> *(Matthew 5:44)*

That is not weakness. It is the rule of the Spirit over the flesh. It takes courage to deny yourself. When Potiphar's wife grabbed Joseph by his garment, he did not allow himself to be dragged down; he broke free and fled. When his brothers bowed before him, Joseph did not humiliate them; he lifted them up and provided for them. That is the strength of one who has forgiven: he renounces the right to revenge because he trusts in a just God.

Forgiving does not make you weak; it makes you free. Bitterness is a shackle you carry, thinking it punishes the other person, when in reality it only chains you to your pain. Grace opens the door. God's justice is not canceled because you forgive; on the contrary, forgiveness allows you to step down from the judge's seat. You do not minimize the offense—you simply place the case in the hands of the only perfect Judge.

THE DARK PART COMES
BEFORE THE GOOD PART

> *"Weeping may endure for a night, but joy comes in the morning".* *(Psalm 30:5)*

Between the pit and the palace, there are nights. Between betrayal and provision, there is silence. And it is there that forgiveness is forged. Darkness is not a disposable paragraph; it is a necessary chapter. Patience produces character, and character produces hope.

Joseph could not fast-forward his story; he had no remote control to skip the suffering. Every scene shaped his heart. The trial was not punishment—it was preparation. In the same way, your process is not an accident; it is a workshop where God refines your soul. To embrace it is to trust that even the night is included in the plan of the day.

AN UNLOCKING THAT RELEASES MIRACLES

Allow me to take you to a story that is less ancient, but just as real. **Rolando** and I were inseparable friends. We dreamed of evangelistic films—dramatizations that would change lives. We shared meals, churches, and projects. We came from different denominations, but our passion for God united us. He even asked me to be his best man, and my family treated him like a son.

The years passed, cities changed, marriages came, and our friendship endured—until a comment, a gesture, a misunderstanding divided us. It was something so small that today I cannot even remember the details. But I nurtured that anger as if it were a rose garden. I did not confront it; I watered it with silence and pride. What began as a thorn became a wall. I blocked his number, his profile, his name from my prayers. I told myself, "I don't need Rolando." Five years passed.

God was blessing me, but every time I sought His presence there was a strange sensation, like a drop that would not evaporate. I asked, "Lord, what is this?" And the conviction came: "Rolando." I laughed. Rolando? Five years later? But the insistence was so strong that I knew it was God. I surrendered to what felt absurd and unblocked his number—nothing more. I closed the phone and went to rest.

A little while later, a message came through: "Saul, I miss you and I love you. I always pray for you." It was Rolando.

My phone nearly slipped from my hands. I replied, I cried, I called him. We talked for hours. We asked each other for forgiveness. I discovered that he had been praying for reconciliation for years, without knowing where I lived. Our forgiveness became a testimony that healed others—friends who had been separated drew close again, families who had been distant embraced. All because the Holy Spirit said, "Unblock," and I obeyed.

I learned that forgiveness sometimes begins with a small gesture that feels ridiculous. Unblocking a contact may seem insignificant—like removing a stopper—but once you do, the river can flow. I learned that pride feeds resentment, but obedience breaks chains. I learned that inside that wound was a decision that changed not only my life, but the lives of many.

INTEGRATED MYTHS, KEYS, AND SIGNS

There are misconceptions that prevent us from forgiving. We believe that forgiveness means forgetting, when in reality it means **remembering with purpose**. We believe that forgiveness means saying what happened was acceptable, when in truth it means naming the evil for what it is and placing it in God's hands. We believe that forgiveness requires immediate trust, when in fact we can establish boundaries until fruit is evident.

We think that if we still feel pain, it must mean we have not forgiven—but a wound can take time to heal even after the decision has been made. We believe forgiveness is unfair, forgetting that divine justice works far better than our resentment. These lies bind us; **truth sets us free.**

- **How Do You Forgive?** Begin by naming the wound. You cannot heal what you refuse to acknowledge. Tell God, "This hurt me." Accept responsibility: you did not choose what was done to you, but you do choose how you respond. Separate forgiveness from restoration: you can forgive someone and still not return to the relationship if there is no safety. Make forgiveness a process: decide today, reaffirm tomorrow, bless with your words, and seek reconciliation when it is wise. Do not let emotions direct your actions; use pain as a signal, not as your master. Ask for help: pray, seek a mentor, and trust the Holy Spirit who speaks. Give thanks for what has already been redeemed; write down the scars that have become testimonies. And bless with your words—speak life instead of curses.

- **Do You Need to Know If You're Still in the Pit?** If you replay the wound over and over without mentioning redemption; if you fantasize about revenge; if it bothers you when the other person prospers; if you distrust everyone because of what one person did; if you gather allies to criticize; if every sermon seems to be for someone else; if the idea of forgiving repulses you— then acknowledge your pit.

Raise your hand. Ask for help. Do not die there. The wound is real, but resentment is optional. And when the opportunity for restoration comes, exercise discernment.

Is there genuine repentance?
Are visible changes evident?
Is there an attempt at restitution?
Is the environment safe?
Do you have peace when you pray?

THE TABLE IN THE MIDDLE OF THE VALLEY

The psalmist said,

> *"You prepare a table before me in the presence of my enemies".*
> *(Psalm 23:5)*

God prepared a table for Joseph in Egypt with his brothers seated before him. He did not wait for them to ask for forgiveness before serving them; he seated them, fed them, and wept with them. Sometimes God calls you to extend the table while the conflict still exists.

Generosity is a spiritual weapon. A banquet of grace can become the signal that awakens repentance. The table does not erase the pain, but it redeems it. Do not wait until everything is resolved to celebrate God's faithfulness. Serve bread now; sometimes that bread is the key to the miracle.

Not Calling Evil Good
Isaiah warns,

> *"Woe to those who call evil good, and good evil".* *(Isaiah 5:20.*

Forgiveness does not mean justifying abuse, lies, or betrayal. The brothers sinned when they sold Joseph. Potiphar's wife sinned when she falsely accused him. The cupbearer failed when he forgot him. Joseph did not say it was right; he said God used it for good.

Do not confuse redemption with complicity. Do not pressure someone to return to a cycle of violence in the name of faith. Forgiveness does not excuse what offends God. Restoration requires repentance and safety. Grace does not twist the truth; truth empowers grace.

Embracing Your Process

Paul wrote that tribulation produces patience, patience produces character, and character produces hope. We want to fast-forward the series of life—skip the uncomfortable episodes and rush past the painful scenes. But every chapter has a purpose.

When I forgave Rolando, I wanted everything to be fixed immediately. And although the message itself was a miracle, the process of healing the relationship took time. Joseph had to wait years to see his brothers again. Forgiveness is a seed planted today that blooms through patience.

Trust the divine Craftsman. His work may be slow or immediate, but it is always secure.

The God of Unexpected Turns

God reveals Himself as the One who "declares the end from the beginning." He delights in surprising us. He takes the improbable and turns it into testimony. Joseph is only one example. Your life also holds unexpected turns waiting to be born.

What seems lost in your story? A relationship, a dream, your self-worth? God knows how to write chapters where there appears to be no ink. But to enjoy those turns, you need a heart free from resentment. Bitterness closes our eyes to miracles. Forgiveness opens them.

WILL YOU FORGIVE?

We have crossed pits, prisons, palaces, and tables. We have watched a young man in a colorful tunic become a governor. We have seen how every wound carried a decision capable of changing destinies. Forgiveness does not erase the past; it redeems it. Forgiveness is inner governance, not weakness. The pit is not your destination; it is a bridge. The table is not set when everything is resolved; it is set in the middle of the valley.

Today, the question is not theoretical; it is personal. **Will you forgive?**

Perhaps that forgiveness has a name and a face: your absent father, your wounding mother, your former spouse, your pastor, your boss, your friend—or yourself. Perhaps it is God, because you did not understand His process. The voice of God whispers to you, "Will you forgive?"

Do not answer with indifference. Do not delay with excuses. The emotion may not be present, but the decision can be. Forgiveness is a key that only you can turn. No one else will do it for you.

Today, I invite you to say yes.
Yes to grace.
Yes to freedom.
Yes to the God of unexpected turns.

Give God permission to take your pit and turn it into a table. Give Him permission to use your wound as a bridge. Give Him permission to redeem your story. And when you respond, remember this: within every wound there is a decision that changes destinies. Your decision today can change your future—and the future of many.

Do you dare?

PRAYER

Lord, You know my wound. Today I choose to forgive [name] for [offense]. I renounce resentment and place the debt in Your hands.

Heal my heart and give me wisdom to set boundaries—or to restore—according to Your will. Thank You for forgiving me first and for teaching me how to forgive. In the name of Jesus. Amen.

CHAPTER 3

WHAT IS THAT IN YOUR HAND?

FROM "WHAT IF...?" TO "THIS IS"

MOSES

THE WEIGHT OF AN IMPOSSIBLE CALLING

For many, Moses is a familiar name; for others, he may be little more than a distant figure from the Bible. Who was this man who would later become the great liberator of Israel?

Moses was born in a dark time. The people of Israel were enslaved in Egypt, and Pharaoh had decreed the death of all Hebrew male infants. In the midst of that threat, his parents hid him for three months, until they could no longer do so. Then his mother prepared a basket, covered it with pitch, and placed him in the Nile River *(Exodus 2:1–3)*. At first glance, it looked like a desperate farewell, but in reality it was the beginning of a divine plan.

God's providence moved Pharaoh's daughter to find the baby and adopt him as her own *(Exodus 2:5–10)*. Thus, Moses grew up in the corridors of power, educated in all the wisdom of Egypt, trained in science, politics, and military strategy *(Acts 7:22)*. He had the resources, the position, and the preparation any leader could dream of. He knew firsthand the suffering of his people, yet he also mastered the language and culture of the most powerful empire of his time.

And yet, the story took an unexpected turn. One day, when Moses saw an Egyptian beating a Hebrew, he intervened and killed him. He thought no one had seen him, but the news spread quickly. Realizing that even his own Hebrew brothers did not recognize him as a leader, he fled to the desert of Midian *(Exodus 2:11–15)*.

There he spent forty years in anonymity—not as a prince, but as a shepherd. His scepter of authority became a shepherd's staff. His influential words in the royal court were replaced by silence in the wilderness. His dreams of greatness seemed to have died.

From a human perspective, Moses appeared disqualified: a fugitive murderer, an aging man without power or army, someone buried in routine. But in God's eyes, that season was not rejection—it was silent training. God was not finishing with Moses; He was forming him.

And it was precisely there, in the middle of the ordinary, that the extraordinary was about to ignite...

THE CALLING AND THE QUESTION THAT CHANGED EVERYTHING

There stood Moses, face to face with a spectacle that defied all logic: a bush on fire that was not consumed. If he had owned a cellphone, he probably would have recorded a viral video for *EgyptTube* titled, "Indestructible Bush Burns for 40 Minutes and Still Intact!" But no—there were no cameras or filters. Just an ordinary man, a silent desert, and a voice that shook eternity.

From that burning bush, God did not only call Moses—He also gave him a mission that sounded like something out of a nightmare:

"So now, go. I am sending you to Pharaoh to bring my people, the Israelites, out of Egypt".

(Exodus 3:10)

The problem is that Moses did not jump for joy or shout, "Amen, here I am!" Instead, he launched into the familiar marathon of excuses that many of us know all too well:

- "Who am I?" (free translation: "I don't qualify")
  (*Exodus 3:11*).

- "What should I say if they ask me?" ("I don't have
  enough answers") (*Exodus 3:13*).

- "They won't believe me" ("My reputation is ruined")
  (*Exodus 4:1*).

- "I am not eloquent" ("I don't have the right skills")
  (*Exodus 4:10*).

- And the final gem: "Please, Lord, send someone else"
  ("I'm out—thanks anyway") (*Exodus 4:13*).

It is ironic: Moses was standing before a bush that would not
burn out, speaking with the living God Himself—yet his mind
was still tangled in insecurity. This reminds us that doubt does
not disappear in the presence of miracles; it is overcome
through faith and obedience.

And right there—when Moses' excuses seemed stronger than
the calling itself—God did not deliver a sermon or outline a
strategic plan. He simply asked a question—simple,
disarming, and final:

"What is that in your hand?" (Exodus 4:2)

The scene freezes. The question echoes: "What is that in your
hand?" Moses looks down, and all he sees is a staff. That
moment was more than a conversation—it was the breaking
point of a story. Because the question was not seeking
information—God already knew what Moses was holding—it
was seeking revelation.

The Lord was saying, "What you already carry, I will use. What you consider insignificant, I will transform. You do not need more; I only need you to surrender what you have."

And just like that, an ordinary piece of wood became the symbol of the extraordinary.

There, in the silence of the desert, the Lord showed Moses signs to strengthen his faith: the staff that turned into a serpent, the hand that became leprous and was healed *(Exodus 4:6–7)*, and the water from the river that could turn into blood *(Exodus 4:9)*.

This was not a public spectacle or a power demonstration before Pharaoh. It was an intimate encounter between God and His servant—a closed-door training session. Before using Moses' hands to part seas, God first had to address the fears within his heart.

And God does the same with us. When you decide to obey, God does not abandon you to uncertainty. He personally confirms your faith with signs that remind you that you are not walking alone. Sometimes those signs are miracles that defy logic; other times, they are doors that open at just the right moment, people who confirm what God has placed in your heart, or a peace so real it dismantles anxiety.

But here is the key: signs do not replace faith. They are a push, a reminder, a spark. Moses saw the staff become a serpent, his own hand become diseased and healed within seconds, and water turn into blood—and still he doubted. That reveals something profound: miracles impress, but they do not necessarily convince.

Faith is not born from the fireworks of power, but from trusting the voice of God that speaks behind them.

In other words: **the burning bush was the laboratory; Egypt would be the stage.**

THE STAFF IN THE HANDS OF GOD

Moses looks down and realizes that what he is holding is… a stick. Yes, a simple staff. Nothing worthy of a museum, nothing impressive at a relic auction. Just a shepherd's staff, worn by the sun and the sand of the desert. It probably even bore the marks of chasing away a stubborn sheep or two.

But God looks at it as if it were the most valuable object on the planet. And then He says:

"Throw it on the ground". (Exodus 4:3)

Moses obeys, and what seemed like a harmless piece of wood turns into a serpent. Imagine the scene: Moses—the future liberator—runs away! Because one thing is having faith, and another very different thing is grabbing a moving snake in front of you.

"Reach out your hand and take it by the tail".

(Exodus 4:4)

That is too much. If you have ever seen a snake, you know that grabbing it by the tail is the worst idea in the world. It is like saying, "Go ahead and bite—I'm giving you a free shot." But here is the key: what seems logical to humans is not always what opens the door to the supernatural.

Moses obeys, and once again, what was a serpent becomes a staff. This moment was not a magic show. It was God teaching him: "Moses, in My hands, the ordinary becomes extraordinary. I do not need more from you than your obedience."

From the Private Courtyard to the Public Stage

What began as a lesson in the desert soon became a public display before Pharaoh. That same staff was raised again and again:

- It struck the waters of the Nile, and they turned to blood *(Exodus 7:20)*.

- It pointed to the land and unleashed plagues (Exodus 8–10).

- Finally, it was lifted over the Red Sea, and the waters were divided in two *(Exodus 14:16)*.

The same staff Moses once used to guide sheep was now guiding an entire nation toward freedom.

The Second Time: At the Red Sea

And here the same question appears again—this time implicitly. Israel is trapped: the sea in front, the army behind, the desert on both sides. The people cry out, Moses prays, and God interrupts him:

"Why do you cry to Me? Tell the children of Israel to go forward. And you, lift up your staff, and stretch out your hand over the sea and divide it..."

(Exodus 14:15–16)

It was as if God were saying, "Moses, I have not changed My strategy. What I placed in your hand is still enough. You do not need another tool, you do not need a sword, you do not need an army. Just lift what I already gave you."

The echo of that first question rang out once more. Only now it was no longer a private test in the desert, but a public act before countless eyes and an impossible sea.

It was not a new method; it was the same faithfulness. God would once again use what was already in Moses' hand.

The Bridge to You

And now the story points directly to you: are you still living in the territory of "what if...?" Or are you ready to step into "this is"?

- This is what God gave you.

- This is enough in His hands.

- This is what He will use to open your sea.

Faith is not fed by hypotheses; it is sustained by certainties. And the greatest certainty you can have is this: God is with you, and what you hold in your hand is enough to begin.

And as this question echoes through history, it reached me as well.

A MIRROR IN MY OWN LIFE

And here I pause. Because speaking about Moses is not only

about a man who lived thousands of years ago. It is like looking into a mirror. I cannot read his doubts without remembering my own. I cannot hear his "what if...?" without also hearing mine, repeated in my mind for years.

I have learned that I, too, am a modern-day "Moses," carrying questions, excuses, and fears. I am 52 years old, and although I grew up in the faith, I have still encountered that whispering voice that says:

- "What if it's already too late for you?"

- "What if you don't have a formal ministry?"

- "What if those who know your past say, 'Who do you think you are?'"

- "What if you never accomplish what you dreamed?"

That question—what if...?—has been my companion for years. But in the middle of that noise, God reminded me of the same thing He told Moses: "What is that in your hand?"

In my case, what I hold is not a staff, but a gift for writing, for creating images, for communicating what God places in my heart. More than a year ago, the Lord moved me to write my first book—and I finished it. In that process, even though I did not understand everything, a desire and clarity were born in me to keep writing. Today, I already have the titles and outlines of eight books in order. Not because I am someone great, but because God has been clear that this is the path I am meant to walk.

Yes, I have studied theology and communications. Yes, I have a background as a graphic artist and as a pastry chef. But I also carry serious mistakes, failures that could have cost me my marriage, decisions I deeply regret. And yet, here I am. And all I can say is that the grace and mercy of God have sustained me to this day.

Recently, in the middle of worship during a service, God confirmed something that still shakes me: this calling to write, to plant His Word in hearts, is His plan for my life. I do not know the details—how these books will be distributed, who will read them beyond my circle, or whether I will ever have the reach of authors I admire. But what I do know is this: God has spoken to me, and this is what I have in my hands. And I will do it.

I may not be the next Max Lucado, nor José Luis Navajo, nor as eloquent as Steven Furtick. But that is not the point. I am Saul Miranda: visual thinker, graphic artist, pastry chef, writer, husband, and father living under the grace of God. What I have in my hands—words, pages, stories—I place before the Great I AM. That certainty redefined my perspective. I no longer walk asking, "What if I fail?" but declaring, "This is what God entrusted to me, and this is what I will give."

And yet, before arriving here, there was a season in my life when I felt stuck. Yes, I prayed. Yes, I attended services when my schedule allowed. I enjoyed God's presence and the peace of salvation. But inside, there was an emptiness I could not fill. I remembered promises and youthful dreams that did not unfold the way I imagined—largely because of my own stubbornness. And over time, that feeling turned into resignation: "Maybe my time has passed. What remains is to pray for my family and make the most of the moments God gives me to encourage someone."

That was not insignificant—I truly valued it—but it was not the echo of the calling that burned in my soul: to leave a mark, to be useful in His hands.

That pause weighed on me. I feared dying without having deeply impacted anyone, passing through life without having made a difference. I felt as though my best years—and my failures—had closed the door to a greater purpose. And in that silence, what once had been a dream began to feel like an impossible memory.

Until the book came.

What felt to me like a simple act of obedience, God used as a key to open something I thought was sealed shut. It was not just creativity; it was life flowing again. Ideas began to emerge—outlines, titles, an urgency to write and share what God had deposited in my heart. In the middle of doubt, I felt a clear confirmation: I can still be useful. Not because of my merits, but because God does not discard what He touches. That moment was a rebirth, proof that God does not waste our hands or our years.

Today I continue to pray with the same conviction: I do not want to pass unnoticed. My desire is that my life would serve, that what I write and share would have impact. I do not seek human recognition; I want to be an instrument in the hands of the Great I AM—even if it is to change just one life a year. And if He chooses to multiply it to many, I am ready for that as well. What matters is that I no longer live paralyzed by "what if…?" but propelled by a "this is" that leads me to obedience.

But even though the staff had already proven its power, the true obstacle was not in the sea—it was in Moses' mind. His hands held a staff; his heart still carried questions. And that is where we enter the territory of "what if…?"

FROM "WHAT IF…?" TO "THIS IS"

Where you see probability, He sees fact. Where you see limitation, He sees purpose. Where you see failure, He sees an opportunity to display His glory. God's "this is" cuts at the root of humanity's "what if…?" That "this is" was not a rebuke; it was direction.

Moses had exhausted all his arguments. He had already laid out his fears, his past, his limitations, and even his difficulty speaking. Every excuse sounded reasonable. Every doubt felt logical. Yet God did not negotiate with any of them. He did not present a new plan, He did not deliver a motivational speech, nor did He allow Moses to remain paralyzed by insecurity. Instead, He confronted him with a simple truth: "This is what you have, and this is what I will use."

That was the turning point. Moses spoke in conditionals: "What if they don't believe me? What if I fail?" But God responded in the present tense, with the certainty of the One who holds all things together:

"This is what I will do. This is who I AM. This is enough, because I will be with you."

That contrast is still alive today. We fill our hearts with hypothetical scenarios:

What if I can't provide for my family? What if I never fulfill my purpose? What if others reject me? What if it's already too late for me?

But while our minds manufacture doubts, the voice of God continues to declare certainties: This is My grace that sustains you. This is My plan that does not depend on your credentials. This is My power, made perfect in your weakness.

The "what if" traps us in an imaginary future shaped by fear. The "this is" plants us firmly in the present of faith.

One drains our energy before we ever act; the other propels us to take steps we would never dare take on our own. Moses discovered that it was never about him, but about the God who was sending him. The staff in his hand had nothing special in itself—but once he obeyed and surrendered it, it became an instrument of miracles.

That same invitation is extended to you. You do not need to resolve every variable in life before you move. You do not need to wait until everything is perfect to begin. You only need to place in God's hands what you already have and believe Him when He says, "This is enough."

That is why this chapter does not end with Moses' excuses or fears, but with the firm voice of God that cuts doubt at its root. It is as if heaven were speaking to you today, repeating the same words that disarmed Israel's liberator: "This is what you have. This is what I will use. This is enough—because I am with you."

And there, between human insecurity and divine certainty, the future is decided. Because when you let go of "what if...?" and embrace "this is," the sea that once seemed immovable begins to open before you.

What happened to Moses is not just ancient history; it is a mirror reminding us that God is still asking the same question today: "What is that in your hand?"

Yours may not be a staff—but there is something God wants to use right now. And if you choose to believe Him, that "this is" will be enough to open your own sea.

In the next chapter, we will see how another servant of God was confronted with a different question—yet just as challenging. Because every calling begins with a voice, but also with a question that changes everything.

PRAYER

Lord, here is what I have in my hand.
It may seem small, but I place it in Yours.

Break within me the "what if...?"
and establish Your "this is."

Give me the courage to obey,
even when my emotions tremble.

Teach me to trust Your presence
more than my own guarantees.

Use who I am and what I have
for Your glory.

In the name of Jesus. Amen.

CHAPTER 4

WHY ARE YOU LYING ON YOUR FACE?

YOU CANNOT CONQUER WHAT GOD PROMISED WHILE HOLDING ON TO WHAT HE FORBADE

JOSHUA

WHEN DEFEAT REVEALS WHAT VICTORY DID NOT

They say there are victories that lift you up, and defeats that reveal you. There are moments when God opens seas and brings down walls—and others when He allows something to fall so you can see what you preferred not to see. This chapter belongs to the second category. It is not a section that celebrates a heroic triumph or a spectacular miracle; it is a story that strips the heart bare. It teaches us that there is no enemy more dangerous to the calling God places on a person than what one chooses to hide.

THE OBEDIENCE THAT BROUGHT DOWN WALLS... AND THE COMMAND THAT COULD NOT BE IGNORED

Before Israel suffered defeat at Ai, before Joshua's bitter weeping, there was a clear command. The battle of Jericho was not won through military strategy or human weapons, but through obedience. God gave unusual instructions: to march around the walls once a day for six days, and on the seventh day to march seven times and shout. The people obeyed.

There was no strength in the arms of the Israelites, but power in the word of God. And the walls of Jericho fell.

Scripture declares it plainly:

> *"So the people shouted, and the priests blew the trumpets. And it happened, when the people heard the sound of the trumpet and the people shouted with a great shout, that the wall fell down flat".*

> *(Joshua 6:20)*

It was not blows or battering rams that brought the walls down; it was obedience.

However, alongside the instructions for the march came a command that many overlook. God warned them: *"But you, by all means abstain from the accursed things... lest you become accursed when you take of the accursed things, and make the camp of Israel a curse, and trouble it"* (Joshua 6:18). The term accursed refers to what is devoted to God—items set apart to be destroyed or consecrated exclusively to Him. In Jericho, God ordered that everything—silver, gold, and vessels of bronze and iron—be consecrated to the Lord's treasury: *"But all the silver and gold, and vessels of bronze and iron, are consecrated to the LORD; they shall come into the treasury of the LORD"* (Joshua 6:19). Nothing was to be taken by the people. By obeying, Israel would not only gain victory; they would also preserve the purity of their relationship with God.

Jericho fell. The nation experienced a supernatural triumph. Joshua's name became known throughout the land. The people witnessed the manifestation of a powerful God—One who opens the Jordan, brings down immovable walls, and honors faith. It was a moment of euphoria and expectation. But the obedience that brings down walls must continue after the victory. And that is where many fail. Success reveals not only the glory of God, but also the human heart's tendency to take what does not belong to it.

FROM JERICHO TO AI: WHEN SUCCESS HIDES A CRACK

The next mission was Ai. At first glance, it was a small town with no extraordinary fortifications—an enemy insignificant compared to Jericho. The spies returned confidently and said, *"Do not let all the people go up, but let about two or three thousand men go up and attack Ai. Do not weary all the people there, for the people of Ai are few" (Joshua 7:3).*

And yet, the men of Ai struck down thirty-six Israelites and chased the rest away. It was Israel who fled, not the enemy. Scripture describes it this way: *"And the men of Ai struck down about thirty-six men, for they chased them from before the gate as far as Shebarim, and struck them down on the descent; therefore the hearts of the people melted and became like water" (Joshua 7:5).*

How does one move from a glorious victory to a shameful defeat? How can the power of God be experienced one day and His absence felt the next? The answer is not found in the strength of the enemy, but in the disobedience of the heart.

Joshua did not understand what had happened. He fell on his face, tore his clothes, and put dust on his head. His cry sounds like ours when things do not go as expected: "Why, Lord? What is happening? Weren't You with us?" In his desperation, Joshua wondered whether the God who opened the Jordan and brought down Jericho had abandoned them. But God had not left; the people had drifted away.

When Joshua expected words of comfort, God responded with a phrase that cut like a sword: *"Get up! Why do you lie thus on your face?" (Joshua 7:10).* This was not divine indifference; it was confrontation. God was not dismissing Joshua's pain—He was exposing a hidden root. The defeat was not due to the enemy's superior strength; it was due to hidden sin.

ACHAN: WHAT WAS SEEN, COVETED, AND BURIED

Achan was the man who violated the divine command. He saw a Babylonian garment, silver, and gold. He coveted them. He took them. He hid them. What many might consider a "small" act altered the destiny of an entire nation. Scripture details the scene: what Achan saw, he desired, and he took. That progression reflects the path of many temptations—first the glance, then the desire, and finally the action.

Sin did not begin when his hands touched the gold, but when his eyes lingered without restraint. The warning in Deuteronomy 7:26 was clear: *"Nor shall you bring an abomination into your house… you shall utterly detest it and utterly abhor it, for it is an accursed thing."* Achan disregarded the warning. He took what was devoted to destruction and buried it beneath his tent. Perhaps he thought the spoil would provide for his family; perhaps he believed he deserved it for the battle they were fighting. But his "reward" brought only death and disaster.

Here is where the private becomes public and the personal becomes communal. Scripture says that *"the children of Israel committed a trespass… for Achan took of the accursed things; so the anger of the LORD burned against the children of Israel"* (Joshua 7:1).

Notice the language: **Israel sinned,** not just Achan. One individual action produced a corporate consequence. Hidden sin always reaches beyond the sinner. What is concealed in secret becomes a seed of destruction for the family, the congregation, and the mission. Achan's disobedience not only removed God's covering; it also cost the lives of thirty-six innocent men. His family, who knew the secret, shared in the judgment. Hidden sin never stays at home—it carries chaos beyond it.

Today, it is difficult for many to understand the severity with which God dealt with Achan. Some read the story and think the punishment was disproportionate. Yet God's judgment was not arbitrary. The Lord had warned that taking what was devoted to other gods would bring a curse upon the camp. Achan ignored the divine word. His action was a deliberate act of rebellion. Moreover, in Israel's earliest conquests, God was establishing principles for the entire nation. The community would learn that **individual sin compromises collective well-being,** and that **holiness is not optional in God's mission.**

OUR "ACCURSED THINGS" TODAY: WHAT WE KEEP HIDDEN IN OUR TENTS

In our lives today, few of us face physical camps and wars, but all of us battle temptations that whisper, "Just look at it. Just touch it. Just take it." The "things devoted to other gods" today are those areas God has asked us to surrender completely: sexual purity, financial integrity, honesty at work, marital faithfulness, holiness in media consumption, care in the words we speak, the management of anger, and our thought patterns. And the accursed things are those practices and habits God calls ungodly, destructive, or harmful.

Achan's garment takes different forms today: pornography consumed in secrecy; inappropriate messages on social media; emotional affairs disguised as innocent friendships; financial corruption accepted as "being smart"; white lies repeated until we believe them; thoughts of hatred or racism hidden behind religious language. Each one, though different, works the same way: you harbor something God said must be destroyed, you think you can control it, you bury it in your tent, and you believe it will not affect your calling. But it does. Deeply.

When God said to Joshua, "I will not be with you anymore unless this remains," He was revealing a profound spiritual reality. The Lord did not withdraw His love nor revoke His promise, but He withheld His backing of the people's endeavors while the accursed thing remained. It was not that God stopped being God to them; it was that sin interrupted the covenant support in that moment. God can tolerate your frailty, but He will not endorse your disobedience. He can cover your mistakes, but He will not bless your secrets. He can walk with you through the process, but He will not march on ground you yourself have contaminated.

In other words, you cannot expect to move forward with God while clinging to what He has already condemned. Hidden sin not only damages your communion with God; it stalls your assignment, cools your passion, distorts your priorities, and contaminates your influence.

This chapter is direct because grace is deep. No one exposes what is hidden to humiliate; God exposes it to heal. Many Christians live for years frustrated and confused about their calling, wondering why doors do not open and why they do not experience the power others seem to have. They attend retreats, fast, serve, and pray—and yet feel stuck. Sometimes the enemy does not need to destroy your faith or silence your prayer; he only needs to convince you to bury something God said must die.

It is possible to sing in the choir, preach sermons, lead a small group, or oversee a ministry while hiding improper things on your phone. It is possible to minister to others while maintaining a secret affair. It is possible to give large offerings while cheating on your taxes. It is possible to help the poor while secretly hating a brother. And it is possible for everything to keep "working" because gifts and callings are irrevocable. But, as happened at Ai, there comes a moment when a lack of integrity produces a fracture. In His grace, God allows that loss to confront us—not to destroy us, but to keep us from continuing forward away from Him.

There is something deeper here: hidden sin distorts our perception of God. After the defeat at Ai, Joshua implicitly accused God of unfaithfulness: "Why... have You delivered us?" What a statement from a leader who had seen the sea open! Unconfessed sin in the community caused Joshua to question the character of God.

That is how it happens with us. When we hide, we begin to perceive God through the lens of our own guilt. We may think God is punishing us unjustly, when in reality He is inviting us to confess. We may feel God has abandoned us, when in truth He is calling us to return. We may believe God is silent, when what has actually happened is that our hearing has been clogged with the very dirt we ourselves have piled up.

WHEN GOD SAYS "GET UP": STEPS TO UNBURY WHAT IS HIDDEN

So what should we do then? **First,** we need the courage to stop and examine our tents. Jesus said it another way: *"Therefore if your hand or your foot causes you to sin, cut it off and cast it from you... And if your eye causes you to sin, pluck it out and cast it from you..."* (Matthew 18:8–9). Not literally, but spiritually: eliminate the cause.

What is in your life that God has already declared accursed? What practice, habit, or relationship have you justified by saying, "This isn't that serious"? The first exit door is brutal honesty—with yourself and with God. This is not about a generic confession ("Forgive me for everything I've done wrong"), but a specific one:

"Lord, I have been watching inappropriate things, lying in my finances, criticizing my brothers, sexually fantasizing about someone who is not my spouse, manipulating people, holding on to resentment, stealing time at work. This is in my tent. I buried it. I give it to You."

> God knows the details, but He wants to hear your confession because **confession breaks the power of secrecy.**

Second, we must ask for help. Temptation thrives in isolation. Achan acted alone and died alone. Scripture teaches: *"Confess your trespasses to one another, and pray for one another, that you may be healed" (James 5:16).* God's direction often comes through godly people He places around you: a pastor, a mentor, a counselor, a spiritual friend.

It is essential to surround yourself with someone you can say to, "This is in my life; I need you to pray with me and help me destroy it." Shame tells us no one will understand; grace tells us others have walked this road and that freedom comes when we bring into the light what is killing us in the dark. A healthy church is not one where no one sins, but one where everyone knows where to go when they do.

Third, help must include spiritual discipline. God did not only expose Achan; He required that what was devoted to other gods be destroyed. It was not symbolic; it was literal. Pornography is not defeated by tears alone, but by filters, radical changes in what you consume, eliminating access, and surrendering total privacy on your devices.

Greed is not overcome by prayer alone, but by sacrificial generosity. Anger is not healed merely by apologizing after an outburst, but by learning to be silent, receiving counsel, and refusing to feed hostile thoughts. Sin is defeated when we put to death what is earthly in us. Grace is not an excuse to leave the cause of our fall untouched; grace gives us the power to amputate what is killing us.

Fourth, ask God for direction. The same God who exposed the sin also guided Israel back to victory. He does not only point out the problem; He provides the solution. Pray like David: *"Search me, O God, and know my heart; try me and know my thoughts; and see if there is any wicked way in me, and lead me in the way everlasting" (Psalm 139:23–24).*

If hidden sin has made you deaf to His voice, He can open your ears again. God speaks through His Word—read the psalms of repentance *(Psalm 32, 51)*, read the epistles that call us to holiness, meditate on Jesus who invites the weary and burdened to find rest. God also speaks through His Spirit— there is an inner whisper that reminds you that you are a child and that you can cry out, "Abba, Father." God speaks through community—sometimes the counsel you need will come at a discipleship table or in a conversation after a service. His direction does not only point away from sin; it points toward the abundant life He has for you.

Fifth, acknowledge that confession does not erase all

consequences, but it does restore the calling. Achan was judged according to the covenant of his time; Jesus bore the judgment for our sins on the cross. Still, decisions have repercussions. A man who confesses adultery must face the work of restoring his marriage. A woman who admits an addiction needs a process of healing. A business owner who confesses fraud must take legal responsibility. Grace does not erase history; it allows us to redeem it.

What matters is that a life restored by God can experience His backing again. Ai was conquered once what was hidden was removed. Your Ai—that next step, that calling, that victory—will be conquered when you allow God to bring to light what you buried.

Finally, remember that this confrontation happens because God loves you too much to let you live from Jericho to Jericho and die in Ai. He called you for more.

God wants your life to be a story of redemption, not tragedy. He wants to use your past—including your failures—to display His grace. He wants your defeats to become testimonies and your secrets to become meeting places with His mercy. He wants you to experience real freedom, the kind that only comes when you are willing to surrender everything.

Shame will keep you hiding. Pride will convince you that you can manage it. The enemy will remind you of your failure so you will run. But the Holy Spirit whispers the same phrase God spoke to Joshua:

"Get up."

Get up, because there is land to conquer.

Get up, because your fall is not your end.

Get up, because this is not about what you buried, but about what Christ unearthed in you when He rose from the dead.

Get up, because the calling still stands.

What is buried in your tent? Only you and God know. It may be pornography, adultery, racial hatred, envy that eats away at you, addictions to alcohol, drugs, or food; toxic self-image fueled by social media; secret gambling; filthy language in your mind that never reaches your lips; idolatry of fame or money; self-pity that keeps you stuck in victimhood; an abortion no one knows about; sexual abuse that marked you and led you to hide pain; deep, unhealed wounds; real anxiety or depression that, without truth and support, end up governing decisions and delaying processes God wants to heal.

This does not mean emotional pain is imaginary or insignificant. On the contrary—it is precisely because it is real that it must be addressed with truth, grace, and accompaniment. When suffering is not processed, it can unintentionally become a barrier to moving forward—not because the person wants to flee, but because they have not yet found a path to healing.

Whatever it is, God has already seen it. You cannot hide anything from the One who sees the depths of the heart. But you can allow Him to dig into the soil of your soul, remove the accursed thing, and plant an altar of obedience in its place. Holiness is not an impossible burden; it is the fruit of walking with the One who purchased your freedom with blood.

Asking for help does not make you weak; it makes you wise. Acknowledging your sin does not make you less spiritual; it makes you human in need of grace. Seeking direction does not mean you distrust God; it means you want to walk exactly where He wants you to walk.

When you decide to unbury what is hidden, you will discover that God not only restores what you lost—He gives you more than you imagined. Israel did not only conquer Jericho and Ai; they possessed the Promised Land. You will not only be free from your secrets; you will become a testimony of grace that overcomes everything. Your defeat will reveal your heart, but your response will define your future.

Do not wait for Ai to strike before examining your tent. Do not believe the lie that you can move forward in your calling without cleaning what is contaminating it. God's voice today does not condemn you; it invites you. It tells you to lift your eyes from the ground, look toward heaven, and confess what you have hidden. God will never ask something of you to shame you; He will ask it because He wants to make you completely free.

This may be the most uncomfortable conversation you have ever had with God. Reading these words may stir memories, shame, or fear. That is okay. Discomfort is a sign that truth is touching areas long anesthetized. Shame signals that God wants to cover you with His forgiveness. Fear is a symptom of having trusted secrecy more than grace. Do not run. Breathe. Pray. And open the door.

When Joshua obeyed and got up, God told him exactly how to proceed: expose the sin, repent, and consecrate the camp again. It was not an instant process, but it was a safe one. Then God spoke again, as He will to you. He said: *"Do not be afraid, nor be dismayed; take all the people of war with you, and arise, go up to Ai"* (Joshua 8:1).

The same voice that confronted him empowered him again. The same hand that allowed the defeat led him to victory. The same presence that withdrew while sin remained returned to march with His people. That is what God will do with you. He will raise you up with renewed purpose, fire in your heart, and authority you did not have before. And when you look back, you will see Jericho, you will see Ai, and you will see the Promised Land—and you will know that every defeat, every confession, and every tear was worth it, because they led you closer to the God who refuses to leave anything buried that could destroy you.

PRAYER

Lord, today I come before You
without masks, without excuses,
and without soil covering what I have buried.

I do not want to keep moving forward
while something hidden blocks Your calling
or Your presence over my life.
Show me what You see.
Point out what I have ignored.
Reveal what my eyes have refused to look at.
Open my hands to release what You have asked me to surrender.

Clean my tent, Lord.
Purify my heart.
Unbury what bound my soul,
what contaminated my path,
what stole my victory,
and what stalled my purpose.
I do not want to take another step

without Your light shining into the deepest places.
I do not want to conquer anything outwardly
while something within is defeating me.

Give me the courage to face what is hidden,
the humility to ask for help,
the boldness to confess,
and the determination to change.

May Your Holy Spirit do in me
what I cannot do on my own:
break hidden chains,
close doors left open in the dark,
and raise me up in holiness
to walk toward what You have prepared.

Lord, today I declare
that nothing in my life will remain buried
outside of Your will.
I will not live divided.
I will not live hidden.
I will not live far from Your presence.

Lift me up, my God—
purified, clean, free,
and ready to move forward
into the land You have set before me.

In the name of Jesus. Amen.

CHAPTER 5
HAVE I NOT SENT YOU?

WHEN YOU DON'T KNOW WHO YOU ARE, YOU WILL DOUBT HOW GOD SEES YOU

GIDEON

THE WHISPER THAT AWAKENS PURPOSE

There are questions God asks not to receive answers, but to reveal hearts. Questions that do not thunder from heaven, but rise from the depths of the soul. Questions that do not seek information, but transformation.

And one of them still echoes through the centuries:

"Have I not sent you?" (Judges 6:14)

That question carries weight. It does not sound like a military command, but like a loving call.
It does not demand—it awakens.
It does not push—it draws.

And when it comes, it does not matter whether you are prepared; what matters is whether you are willing to listen.

THE MAN WHO WAS HIDING FROM HIS CALLING**

Israel was living under oppression. The Midianites invaded their fields, destroyed their crops, and the people had grown accustomed to loss. Fear had become part of daily routine. And in the middle of that cycle of defeat, a young man named Gideon decided to hide a little wheat—to save something from what the enemy had not destroyed.

"Now the Angel of the LORD came and sat under the terebinth tree which was in Ophrah, which belonged to Joash

the Abiezrite, while his son Gideon threshed wheat in the
winepress, in order to hide it from the Midianites".

(Judges 6:11)

A winepress was not a place to thresh wheat. It was a pit in
the ground where grapes were pressed—no wind, no visibility,
no space. A hiding place. And that is where God found him.

God has a strange habit of showing up where we least expect
Him. He does not look for us in the temple, but in the place
where our purpose is hiding. He does not call from a platform,
but from within our fear.

And there, in that corner of insecurity, God speaks to him
about his future:

"The LORD is with you, you mighty man of valor".

(Judges 6:12)

FACE TO FACE WITH DOUBT

What is striking about this encounter is not only what Gideon
heard, but what he saw. The text says that "the Angel of the
LORD came and sat"—this was not a vision or an inner voice;
it was a visible manifestation.

Gideon had before his very eyes the messenger of the same
God who brought Israel out of Egypt—the God he had heard
about since childhood. And yet... he doubted.

What an irony: he stood face to face with the God of the
stories, and still felt unworthy.

Sometimes we do not doubt God because we fail to believe in

Him, but because we fail to believe He can use us. Gideon did not question God's power; he questioned his own value. What he thought about himself weighed more than what God thought about him.

And even with that doubt, the LORD waited for him. He allowed Gideon to go and prepare an offering—to slaughter the young goat, bake the bread, and bring it back.

What patience God shows! He did not say, "Hurry up," but rather, "Present it." The fire did not fall until Gideon returned, and that reveals something profound:

> God does not reject your process; He waits for your surrender.

THE IDENTITY CRISIS

Imagine Gideon lifting his head—confused, perhaps even letting out a nervous laugh.

"Brave? Me? Lord, I'm just trying to survive."

That is the response of anyone who has spent too long defining themselves by what they have suffered.

Scripture does not give us many details about Gideon before this moment. We are not told his age, his appearance, or his temperament. We are told only one thing—and it is enough: he did not feel sufficient. And that is the key.

There are people who do not run from God out of rebellion, but out of low self-worth. Gideon was not living in sin; he was paralyzed by a distorted identity.

THE DISTORTION OF THE MIRROR

We live in a generation that has learned to look at itself through broken mirrors. We see ourselves through the opinions of others, the filters of social media, the numbers of approval or rejection. We publish edited versions of our lives, and when others applaud that image, we assume the reflection is real. But identity is not built on likes; it is anchored in truth.

Over time, many have come to recognize a profound reality:

Human identity is shaped by the voice it listens to most.

Not so much by what a person does, but by who gives them a name.

When the soul loses its reference point in God, it begins to define itself by substitute voices—other people's expectations, imposed labels, past failures, or constant comparison. Those voices slowly take the place that only the Word of God was meant to occupy.

And that is exactly what happened to Gideon.

He heard so often that his people were weak, that his family was the smallest, that he eventually believed it himself. What he heard from his surroundings became louder than what God had already declared over him.

The voice you listen to most will eventually define who you believe you are.

THE BATTLE FOR MY NAME

I spent years looking at myself through a broken mirror without realizing it. Not because someone else shattered it—I was the one who kept breaking it, piece by piece, with thoughts that did not come from God.

From a young age, I grew up surrounded by nicknames. Some were jokes, others were hidden arrows. And the most cruel ones weren't even real. They were words I imagined people thought about me. Looks I interpreted as judgment, even when no one had said a thing.

I lived on edge, hypersensitive, constantly trying to decipher whether someone was laughing at me or comparing me to others. It was like living in a room full of whispers—most of them coming from my own mind. And those whispers slowly carved a fragile identity.

Speaking in public terrified me. Sharing an idea felt dangerous. Creating something new seemed impossible. Exposing myself was unthinkable. And without realizing it, I developed a constant habit: hiding. Hiding my thoughts, my talents, and my dreams. Hiding from others. Hiding from myself.

Even My Name Felt Heavy

Even my name felt heavy to me. Saul. A beautiful name—"asked of God." But I turned it into a burden. Because it also reminded me of the king who was rejected, and without realizing it, that became an emotional echo inside me. It was as if my own name whispered a false verdict: "God is not pleased with you."

No one ever told me that. But my mind, my wounds, and my insecurities repeated it until I believed it.

That shy child, that teenager who didn't like what he saw in the mirror, that young man who was afraid of his own voice— he didn't know who he was. Until one day, exhausted from hiding from everyone and from myself, I decided to surrender to God.

And He didn't transform me by changing what I saw in the mirror, but by changing the voice behind the mirror. He didn't remove my fears; He took me by the hand and showed me they did not define my purpose. He didn't erase my insecurities; He showed me that even with them, He could still use me. He didn't change me overnight, but He began to heal me—word by word, thought by thought.

Now when I look back, I'm amazed. Who would have thought that the quiet young man would one day lead choirs?

Who would have imagined that the fearful boy would end up creating, writing, teaching, leading? Who would have said that someone who couldn't stand his own reflection would one day find his true identity in God?

Today I know something I didn't know then: God never spoke about me the way I spoke about myself. He never doubted what He placed inside me, even when I did. And that changes everything.

And I understood something that transformed my life: You are not who others said you were. You are not who you thought you were. You are not who fear tried to convince you that you were. You are who God says you are.

He did not make a mistake with me. And He did not make a mistake with you. And to remind me of that, His Word embraced me with this truth:

> *"Put on the new man which was created according to God, in true righteousness and holiness".*
>
> *(Ephesians 4:24)*

THREE MIRRORS OF IDENTITY

1. **What I Think About Myself.** This mirror is full of
   cracks. It reflects the past, mistakes, and fears. It tells
   you, "You can't," "you're not enough," "you've already
   failed too much." And while you look into it, you think
   you are being humble, but in reality, you are believing
   a lie. It is not humility to deny what God has affirmed.
   *"For You formed my inward parts; You covered me in my
   mother's womb. I will praise You, for fearfully and
   wonderfully are Your works; I am wonderfully made, and my
   soul knows it very well"* (Psalm 139:13–14). God did not
   make a mistake with you. Your story may have errors,
   but your design does not.

2. **What Others Think About Me.** This is the loudest
   mirror. We spend our lives trying to reflect someone
   else's light, even though it does not belong to us. We
   want to please, to fit in, to be accepted. And when we
   fail to do so, we think we are worth less. But human
   opinion is volatile; today it celebrates you, tomorrow it
   cancels you. *"For man looks at what is before his eyes, but
   the LORD looks at the heart"* (1 Samuel 16:7). When you
   allow the gaze of others to define your value, you end
   up performing for the wrong audience. And like
   Gideon, you hide in a winepress trying to save a
   reputation, not a purpose.

3. **What God Says About Me.** This is the only mirror that
   does not change. It does not break, it does not rust, it
   does not update with trends. It is eternal. In it, you do
   not see your past; you see your calling. *"But you are a
   chosen generation, a royal priesthood, a holy nation, His own
   special people"* (1 Peter 2:9). When you look into that
   mirror, you discover that your value does not depend
   on what you do, but on who chose you. That is where
   freedom begins. You cannot discover your purpose
   until you embrace your true identity.

WHEN THE CALLING COLLIDES WITH LOW SELF-ESTEEM

Gideon's problem was not a lack of faith in God; it was a lack of faith in himself. That is why God did not speak to him about the enemy, but about his strength.

"Go in this your strength..." (Judges 6:14)

God did not motivate him; He commissioned him. He did not flatter him; He activated him. And that is exactly what He does with all of us who have ever doubted our calling.

Heaven is not waiting for you to overcome your insecurities in order to use you. God uses you to overcome them. The sending does not come after the healing; the healing happens in the sending.

God does not send you when you are ready; He sends you so you can discover that you already were.

THE VOICE THAT REDEEMS

God's voice does not only correct; it redeems. When He speaks to you, He does not describe your present—He awakens your purpose. That is the essence of calling: identity redeemed by the voice of God.

"No fear, for I have redeemed you; I have called you by your name; you are Mine".

(Isaiah 43:1)

Every time God speaks your name, He reminds you of who you are. And while the enemy tries to define you by your failure, God renames you from your destiny.

Gideon was called before winning a battle, before raising an army, before believing in himself.

And the same is true for you. God does not call you for what you do, but for what He deposited in you. The voice of God is not trying to convince you to do something; it is reminding you of who you are while you do it.

THE CLAIM OF WEAKNESS

When God told Gideon, "Go in this your strength," he must have thought, "What strength, Lord? I can barely find the courage to thresh wheat in a pit!"

> *"And he said to Him, 'Oh my Lord, how can I save Israel? Indeed my clan is the weakest in Manasseh, and I am the least in my father's house.'"*
>
> *(Judges 6:15)*

Gideon did what we all do when God calls us: he pulled out the list of excuses. Some pull out a scroll; others, a full thesis.

And we should not judge him, because you and I have done the same:

- "Lord, I don't have time."

- "Lord, I don't have talent."

- "Lord, I don't have the resources."

And God responds with the same eternal calm:
"But you have Me."

> *Sometimes it seems that our prayers are arguments between an architect and a building that does not want to be built.*

MAKE PEACE WITH YOUR STRENGTH

Gideon did not have a strength problem; he had a problem with his strength. He did not know how to use it, accept it, or see it as something divine. He was strong, but his mind had not yet believed it.

The problem is not your weakness; it is that you became friends with it and enemies with your strength. And that is many of us: experts at describing what we are not. We look in the mirror and can list our flaws better than our virtues.

We have turned self-criticism into a form of humility.

But humility is not denying who you are; it is aligning yourself with God's truth about you. Humility is not thinking less of yourself; it is thinking more about what God can do with you.

WHEN YOU BECOME YOUR OWN OBSTACLE

Some enemies do not come with spear or sword; they come with thoughts. Those thoughts that say, "You're not ready," "you already tried," "you're not enough." Gideon was surrounded by enemies on the outside, but the most dangerous one was inside him. And that is where many people get stuck.

God gives you a dream, a word, a calling, but the greatest

battle is not outside—it is in your mind. The enemy does not stop you with chains, but with doubts, and you end up sabotaging what God intended to bless.

Sometimes the enemy does not defeat you; you surrender before the fight even begins.

THE WAR OF THE MIND

If Gideon's mind were a WhatsApp group chat, it would have two contacts who never stop texting him.

One is named Fear, and the other is God.

The problem is that Fear always texts first and sends long voice messages: "Look, you can't do this, you're the youngest, no one will listen to you." And when God finally sends His message, it sounds softer, shorter, but truer:

"You are brave, I am sending you, I am with you." And there is Gideon, reading both messages, with his finger hovering over the phone, not knowing which one to answer first. Because that's what we do; in church we say "amen," but once we leave, we open the fear chat again.

And the worst part is that sometimes we mute God and then say He doesn't answer.

"For as he thinks in his heart, so is he".

(*Proverbs 23:7*)

If what you think about yourself does not align with what God says, you will always live frustrated between what you could be and what you believe you are.

The enemy does not need to destroy you; he only needs to distract you from who you are.

There are people who live their spiritual life as if they were walking with the brakes on. They have direction, they have a destination, but they do not move because they are afraid to move.

And the problem is not a lack of ability, but a fear of movement. God already gave them the map, but they are still waiting for the spiritual traffic light to turn green when He already said a long time ago, "Move forward!"

Others are like a lamp with powerful light, but with the switch turned off. They have power, but they do not let it shine. And while they pray for "more anointing," God is simply waiting for them to turn on what He already placed inside them.

Your potential is not activated when you understand everything, but when you decide to move forward.

THE SPIRITUAL IMPOSTOR SYNDROME

Have you ever felt like you don't deserve what God has said about you? As if He chose the wrong person. As if you were occupying a place that does not belong to you. That is called impostor syndrome—and spiritually, we suffer from it more than we admit.

There are people who pray, serve, preach, or sing, and still feel like they do not qualify. But the truth is that none of us qualifies—that is why there is grace.

"Not that we are sufficient of ourselves to think of anything as being from ourselves, but our sufficiency is from God".

(2 Corinthians 3:5)

God did not make a mistake with you. You did—but He did not.

STOP FIGHTING YOUR REFLECTION

Gideon was fighting with the image he saw. And many of us live the same way: arguing with who we are, like someone who looks in the mirror and refuses to accept what they see. But God does not invite you to fight with yourself, nor to convince yourself by your own strength, but to surrender to what He sees in you.

There is no peace until you make peace with your purpose. There is no rest until you stop hiding your strength behind sanctified excuses. Obedience does not begin when you understand the calling, but when you accept who is calling you.

WHEN HEAVEN CORRECTS YOU WITH TENDERNESS

What is beautiful about the story is that God does not grow tired of reaffirming him. He does not shout at him, He does not shame him, He does not leave him alone.

He says to him:

"Surely I will be with you, and you shall defeat the Midianites as one man".

(Judges 6:16)

God does not argue with your insecurities; He dissolves them with His presence. And that is what transforms Gideon—not a strategy, but a voice. A voice that convinces him that he is not alone.

The presence of God does not only accompany you; it convinces you.

Perhaps you have been serving for years, yet you still struggle to believe that God can use you beyond what you already know. Perhaps you stopped dreaming because someone made you doubt yourself. Or maybe you became accustomed to surviving in the winepress—comfortable, safe, limited.

Today God asks you again:

"Am I not sending you?"

Not to humiliate you, but to remind you that you were made for more. Not to expose you, but to send you.

You were not born to hide in what you fear, but to walk in what you believe.

Gideon did not change in one day, and neither will you. But change begins when you stop arguing with the voice of God. Make peace with your strength. Make peace with what God has already said about you.

Because it is not arrogance to believe God when He says He

has sent you; it is obedience. Because when God sends, He also backs it up.

The calling is not debated; it is answered.

TEARING DOWN THE ALTARS THAT HIDE YOUR IDENTITY

Before raising a sword, Gideon had to raise courage. And his first mission was not against Midian, but against his own past.

God commanded him to tear down the altar of Baal that belonged to his father and to cut down the Asherah pole. At night, fearful yet determined, Gideon obeyed.

Because before conquering the enemy on the outside, he had to tear down the enemy on the inside: inherited idolatry, tradition that kept him enslaved to an identity that was not his own. No one can live out a new identity without breaking down old altars.

Sometimes those altars are not statues, but habits, thoughts, or voices that we continue to worship without realizing it. They are things that make us feel safe, but prevent us from seeing who we truly are in God.

And when the people woke up and saw the altars destroyed, they called him "Jerubbaal," which means "the one who contends with Baal." That new name did not come from God, but from people. It was a mix of mockery and respect—an alias that marked what he had done, but not necessarily who he was.

There are names people give you because of your mistakes, others because of your victories. Some confine you, others elevate you. But none of them define what God has already spoken over you.

BE CAREFUL NOT TO CONFUSE YOUR NICKNAME WITH YOUR PURPOSE

Nicknames, praise, or criticism can shape your mind more than you realize. Gideon had to learn to keep believing what God had said about him, even when people called him by another name.

God did not see him as Jerubbaal...

God continued to see him as a "mighty man of valor".

(Judges 6:12)

And when you finally decide to say "yes," doubt does not disappear—but a patient God appears, confirming, reducing, and breathing life into the call.

THE GOD WHO DOES NOT MAKE MISTAKES
The Fleece and the Confirmations

Gideon did not reject the calling, but he needed assurance. He asked for signs, one after another, seeking confirmation that it was truly God who was sending him.

First, he brought an offering: a young goat, unleavened bread, and broth. The angel touched the meat with his staff, and fire rose from the rock and consumed the offering.

That was the first confirmation: fire upon what had been

offered. There Gideon understood that he was not speaking with an ordinary messenger. But later, when God commanded him to gather an army, fear returned. So he asked for another sign: the famous fleece of wool.

And here it is important to clarify something. When the Bible speaks of a "fleece," it is not referring to a coin, but to a piece of freshly cut sheep's wool; a soft, absorbent piece, commonly used in everyday tasks at that time. Gideon took it as a symbol of testing: something simple, something with no power in itself, yet capable of revealing God's action.

> *"Look, I shall put a fleece of wool on the threshing floor; if there is dew on the fleece only, and it is dry on all the ground, then I shall know that You will save Israel by my hand, as You have said".*

(Judges 6:37)

And God did it. The next morning, the fleece was soaked and the ground was dry. But the human mind—and the fearful heart—always wants a second opinion.

So Gideon asked for the opposite test:

> *"Do not let Your anger burn against me; I will speak but once more: let me test, I pray, just once more with the fleece; let it now be dry only on the fleece, but on all the ground let there be dew".*

(Judges 6:39)

And God, in His infinite patience, did it again.

That wool, that seemingly insignificant piece, became the place where Gideon learned something essential: that faith is not about understanding God, but about learning to trust how He responds.

Every drop of dew was a word, every soaked fiber was a heavenly affirmation: "Yes, it was I who called you."

Each test was a confirmation, but also a lesson: God is not offended by your insecurities if you seek Him sincerely. He can work with your doubt as long as you remain willing to obey.

God is not bothered by your questions; He is glorified when you invite Him to answer them.

When Doubt Knocks Again

After all the signs, words, and promises, Gideon is still trembling. And if we are honest, we understand him. Because believing once is easy; continuing to believe every day—that is the hard part.

He had seen the fire rise from the rock and consume the offering, he had heard the voice, he had felt the presence. But when the moment to act arrived, doubt returned—an uncomfortable visitor that always arrives unannounced.

And here is where many of us resemble him.

We receive a word, we cry during worship, we feel fire—but when we leave the temple, reality cools us down. Fear knocks at the door and asks:

"What if you were wrong?"

Doubt is not the end of your faith; it is the point where you decide whom you trust more.

The Reduced Army

With the signs fulfilled, Gideon gathered his army: thirty-two thousand men ready to fight.

It looked like the beginning of a great victory!

But God had other plans.

> *"And the LORD said to Gideon, 'The people who are with you are too many for Me to give the Midianites into their hands, lest Israel claim glory for itself against Me, saying, "My own hand has saved me.'"*
>
> *(Judges 7:2)*

So the first reduction came:

"Tell whoever is fearful to return "

And twenty-two thousand left. Only ten thousand remained. God looked and said, "They are still too many." And He took them down to the river to test them again.

Only three hundred men were chosen—those who drank water without losing alertness, attentive and watchful. God does not seek multitudes; He seeks willing hearts.

The lesson was clear: it was not about the size of the army, but the quality of faith. God wanted Gideon to understand that victory does not depend on numbers, but on His presence.

How many times has God also reduced your resources, your support, your "armies"? Not to leave you alone, but to show you that He is enough.

God sometimes removes what confuses your dependence.

The Enemy's Dream

"And when Gideon had come, there was a man telling a dream to his companion, and he said:

'Behold, I had a dream: to my surprise, a loaf of barley bread tumbled into the camp of Midian; it came to a tent and struck it so that it fell and overturned, and the tent collapsed.'"

(Judges 7:13)

A loaf of barley bread. Nothing heroic, nothing glorious. Something common, simple, inexpensive. But in the hands of God, what is simple becomes unstoppable.

The enemy was dreaming about the symbol of Gideon's victory, while Gideon was still doubting himself.

Can you imagine that?

While you question whether you can, hell is already nervous because it knows you will.

Sometimes the enemy believes in your calling more than you do.

THE ROLLING BREAD

God shows Gideon that victory would not come with swords, but with something as ordinary as bread. Because what the world calls "common," God calls an "instrument."

That rolling bread represents a faith that no longer walks in fear, but rolls with purpose.

And you, reader, are that bread.

You are that dough that was crushed, fermented, placed into the fire, and now rolls forward, driven by the wind of the Spirit. Nothing attractive, nothing perfect, but prepared by the hands of the Master.

God does not use what shines; He uses what is willing.

From Insignificant to Unstoppable
Barley bread was the food of the poor. Gideon saw himself as the least in his father's house. Nothing matched the logic of victory. But that is what grace does: it turns the ordinary into the supernatural.

> *"God has chosen the foolish things of the world to put to shame the wise, and God has chosen the weak things of the world to put to shame the things which are mighty".*
>
> *(1 Corinthians 1:27)*

That rolling bread knocks down tents just as your small decisions of faith knock down invisible mountains. You do not need to be great to overcome; you need to be guided.

It is not about the size of the bread, but about the power of the wind that drives it.

The Sign of Courage
After hearing the dream, Gideon did not ask for another sign. For the first time, he worshiped.

> *"So it was, when Gideon heard the telling of the dream and its interpretation, that he worshiped".*
>
> *(Judges 7:15)*

That marks the change. The same man who once hid in the winepress now bows in worship. Before, he feared losing; now, he fears disobeying. That is true transformation.

Worship does not begin when everything goes well, but when your heart chooses to believe before it sees.

THE GOD WHO DOES NOT MAKE MISTAKES

God never made a mistake with Gideon, even though Gideon doubted himself many times. And He did not make a mistake with you either.

He knew all your fears before calling you. He knew your falls, your mistakes, your insecurities, and even so He said, "I am sending you."

Because His calling does not depend on your perfection, but on His purpose. God did not choose you because you were already a finished work, but because He trusts what He Himself placed inside you. Scripture affirms this clearly: God chooses the foolish and the despised to shame the strong, so that no one may boast before Him *(1 Corinthians 1:27–29)*. Not because He sees weakness as virtue, but because His power is perfected in dependence. If God did not trust His creation, He would not have entrusted Adam with the care of Eden. If God did not trust what He forms, He would not call shepherds, fugitives, or the fearful to change history. When God calls, He is not gambling; He is affirming His design.

When the Fire Burns Again

There are people who once walked with God, who were used with power, who spoke with fire, who prayed with authority, but allowed their identity to grow cold.

They accepted a false version of themselves. They exchanged the voice of God for the applause of people, or for the silence of weariness. And the enemy convinced them to stay there—satisfied with the memory, dim in appearance, comfortable in an old version of themselves.

But today God says to you:

"I did not leave you on pause; I was preparing you."

If you were once bread in God's oven, do not resign yourself to being dough without purpose. Roll again. Believe again. Say again, "Yes, Lord, here I am."

There is a fire that does not go out; it is only waiting for your obedience to burn again.

The Inner Victory

Gideon did not only defeat the Midianites. He defeated the voice that told him he could not. His greatest enemy did not fall on the battlefield; it fell in his mind.

And that is your battlefield as well. Every time you choose to believe God over fear, you win a war the enemy will never see. Faith is not always measured in shouts or miracles; sometimes it is measured in the simple act of saying, "Yes, Lord."

Heaven does not applaud when you stand out; it applauds when you obey.

THE ECHO OF THE QUESTION

"Did I not send you?" That question does not expire. It was not only for Gideon. It is the voice that continues to resonate in every soul that has ever felt incapable.

And that voice does not push you; it reminds you. It reminds you that you were not designed to hide, but to advance. That you were not called to please, but to obey. That you were not formed to remain in the winepress, but to lead battles that set others free.

> *God's calling does not expire when you doubt; it is reactivated when you obey.*

PRAYER

Lord, thank You because Your voice reaches me even when I do not know who I am. Thank You because You see in me something I forgot to see, and You call me by my name, not by my failures.

Today I choose to make peace with who I truly am in You. I no longer want to define myself by fear, by the past, or by what others have said. Teach me to see myself as You see me: redeemed, courageous, and sent.

If You send me, I will go. Even if I tremble, even if I doubt, even if I am still learning how to believe. Because if You call me, I can no longer hide.

Make me roll like that bread: simple, yet full of identity, purpose, and faith. Amen.

CHAPTER 6

WHY HAVE YOU DESPISED THE COMMANDMENT OF THE LORD?

THE END OF YOUR STORY IS WRITTEN BY GRACE, NOT BY YOUR SHAME

DAVID

A CHOSEN KING, YET HUMAN

I have no problem admitting it: **David is one of my favorite characters in the Bible.** Not only because God chose him while he was a simple shepherd—an adolescent caring for sheep in Bethlehem—but because his story shows that God's greatness can spring from human smallness. David did not seek the throne; he was anointed in secret and continued serving his father.

When he faced Goliath, it was not for fame, but out of zeal for the name of the LORD. And even after being anointed as king, he knew how to wait for his time. Saul was still on the throne, and David, instead of seizing power, remained humble. His relationship with Jonathan, Saul's son, was one of sincere loyalty; he loved the son of the man who wanted to kill him.

> *"And Jonathan and David made a covenant, because he loved him as his own soul".*
>
> *(1 Samuel 18:3–4)*

Later, when he was already king, he sought out Mephibosheth, Jonathan's disabled son, to show him mercy.

> *"Is there still anyone left of the house of Saul, that I may show him kindness for Jonathan's sake?"*
>
> *(2 Samuel 9:1)*

All these scenes portray him as a man sensitive to God and to people. That combination of courage, humility, and mercy is inspiring.

But the Bible does not hide his shadows. After so many victories, David committed willful sins that cannot be attributed to an "attack of the enemy." It was the weakness of a heart that had fallen asleep in comfort. The account of Bathsheba and Uriah, in 2 Samuel 11, places him at the height of power and at the same time at the depths of moral failure. God sent the prophet Nathan to confront him with a piercing question:

"Why have you despised the word of the LORD?"

(2 Samuel 12:9)

That question is the axis of this chapter. How can someone so loved and used by God despise His word? What happens when the hero becomes the villain of his own story? And perhaps more crucially, what does this teach us about our own weaknesses and the grace that continues to pursue us?

THERE ARE QUESTIONS... AND THEN THERE ARE QUESTIONS

God loves to teach through questions. "Where are you?" He asked in Eden—not to locate Adam geographically, but to lead him to recognize his moral deviation. "What are you doing here, Elijah?" was the question in the cave at Horeb that pulled him out of self-pity. *"Whom shall I send, and who will go for Us?"* provoked Isaiah's surrender to the mission. These questions awaken purpose, mobilize, and activate faith. But there are others that strip us bare: Nathan told a parable about a rich man who stole a poor man's lamb, and when David became indignant, the prophet looked him in the eyes and asked:

"Why have you despised the word of the LORD?"

(2 Samuel 12:9)

There are no compliments here, no heroic invitations—there is confrontation. Why does God confront us this way? Wouldn't it be easier to ignore our failures? The answer is that God loves us too much to leave us in self-deception.

The questions that hurt us are the ones that heal us.

Perhaps you have felt something similar: you read a passage, hear a sermon, or a trusted person says to you, "Why do you keep walking this path if you know it is destroying you?" These are questions that pierce the armor. And the most uncomfortable part: many times we know the answer is not "because the devil forced me," but "because I let myself be carried away." It is easier to attribute everything to spiritual attacks than to acknowledge our disordered desires. That honesty is part of healing.

An interesting detail is that before Nathan asked the question, he allowed David to pronounce judgment on the parable. Have you noticed how often we tend to be strict, severe, or critical of others' mistakes, but when it comes to ourselves, we are more lenient, tolerant, or even justificatory? God allows us to see our hypocrisy so that, like David, we say:

"I have sinned against the LORD". (2 Samuel 12:13)

It is there, in acknowledging the truth, that liberation begins.

SHAME THAT BECOMES A CHAIN

David sinned voluntarily. The Bible does not speak of a demon of lust stalking him on the rooftop; it speaks of an idle king who saw something he should not have seen and chose to act. After sleeping with Bathsheba, his immediate reaction was to hide. Shame entered the scene.

> *"While I kept silent, my bones grew old, Through my groaning all the day long. For day and night Your hand was heavy upon me; My vitality was turned into the drought of summer".*
>
> *(Psalm 32:3–4)*

The words are graphic: bones grow old, life dries up. Hidden sin has a physiological and emotional effect. The hand of God weighs not as vengeance, but as a reminder that something is wrong. When we hide, we wither.

Have you ever felt like that? It may not be adultery, but perhaps envy you never confessed, resentment you secretly nurture, the "small" lie no one knows about. All hidden sin becomes a burden. What is interesting is that shame produces two opposite reactions: it either drives us to cover things up even more, or it pushes us to confess. In David's case, at first it was the former. He summoned Uriah so it would appear the child was his; then he sent him to his death. Shame led him to manipulation and murder. There is no "Satan made me do it" here; there is a heart choosing the easier path.

Moreover, shame has the ugly habit of multiplying. What began with one man's covetous glance ended up affecting an entire kingdom. When Amnon, David's son, raped his sister Tamar, the father remained silent. How could he correct something he himself had done? Shame silenced his authority. Absalom, Tamar's brother, killed Amnon and later conspired against his father. The sword prophesied by Nathan did not depart from his house.

> *"Now therefore, the sword shall never depart from your house..."*
>
> *(2 Samuel 12:10)*

PASSIVITY AT THE DOOR
Opened the Entrance to Chaos

Shame also steals your identity. *"My sin is always before me" (Psalm 51:3)*, says the psalmist. Suddenly, in your mind, you are no longer "a child of God," but "the one who did that thing." Shame baptizes you with new names: adulterer, traitor, hypocrite. This is how the enemy operates: he tempts you and then accuses you. The problem is that if you believe him, you accept a name God never gave you. You replace the voice of the Father who says, "you are loved," with the voice of the accuser who whispers, "you are defective."

One aspect we often forget is that shame does not travel alone. It drags pain, silence, and distance with it. God can forgive in an instant, but the people we love need time to heal. Confession does not erase the memories of a betrayed wife or of children who saw their father live a double life. That is why it is important to understand that vertical restoration (with God) and horizontal restoration (with people) do not happen simultaneously or at the same pace. When we wound others, we cannot demand that they respond as God does.

God forgets our sins; our loved ones remember them, and those scars become part of the story. Acknowledging this is not a lack of faith; it is respect for the humanity of others.

So how do we break that chain? Confession is the first blow. David experienced it:

> "My sin I acknowledged to You, and my iniquity I have not hidden. I said, 'I will confess my transgressions to the LORD,' and You forgave the iniquity of my sin".
>
> (Psalm 32:5)

To confess is not merely to unload the conscience; it is to call sin by its name and take responsibility. There is relief that comes from bringing into the light what is killing us in the dark. Confessing to God brings forgiveness; confessing to those we have hurt begins a process of restoration. But be careful: confession does not magically erase consequences. David was forgiven, but his son died; his family was left fractured. In the same way, when someone confesses infidelity, trust is not restored in a single day. It will require patience, boundaries, counseling, and much grace. God removes guilt, but He does not erase the scars others carry. That tension is part of the Christian walk—celebrating forgiveness without evading responsibility.

THE SHEPHERD'S VOICE THAT CORRECTS AND RESTORES

In the midst of the disaster caused by his sin, David discovered something: **God not only confronts him, He also shepherds**

him. The same One who took him from the pastures to face Goliath now calls him to repentance. Hebrews affirms:

> *"For whom the LORD loves He chastens, and scourges every son whom He receives".*
>
> *(Hebrews 12:6)*

This breaks our idea of God as a distant judge who only issues verdicts. God corrects because He loves. Discipline is not punishment; it is therapy. He straightens us when we have bent the path.

Do you remember Psalm 23? *"The LORD is my shepherd; I shall not want."* David wrote it before his fall, but that truth remained true afterward. The Shepherd does not abandon the wounded sheep; He heals it and guides it back. Even after his adultery, David was shepherded. The correction came through Nathan, but the restoration came from God Himself. God's grace is so radical that He continues to call us even after we have despised His word. Is that not astonishing? Many of us, if we were in God's place, would have canceled David. God, instead, confronted him, disciplined him, and restored him.

The rod and the staff do not only comfort; they also correct. We love to hear that God leads us "to green pastures," but we forget that, to get there, He sometimes uses the rod. The rod drives away wolves and also gently strikes the sheep that is approaching the cliff. Accepting God's correction is an act of trust. It means admitting that He knows better. It is recognizing that not every obstacle comes from the devil. When your spiritual leader or your spouse confronts you, can you discern whether that voice comes from the Shepherd? Not every correction is an attack. Sometimes the "no" you receive is the rod of love.

It is important to highlight a truth: **God's correction is perfect, but we are human.** When we confess, God forgives and chooses not to remember our sin *(1 John 1:9)*. But those around us do remember. This creates a complex process: spiritually we are clean, but relationally there are scars. An unfaithful husband may experience God's peace and, at the same time, face the distrustful gaze of his wife. A leader who abused authority may receive divine forgiveness, but will need time to regain credibility. Grace removes guilt before God; trust before people is rebuilt with consistency. Meanwhile, inner freedom and outer fragility coexist. It is an uncomfortable space where we learn humility.

To accept the rod is to embrace grace. Some want grace without discipline; others want discipline without grace. Scripture gives us both. David experienced forgiveness and consequences. His son died, but he was not discarded as king. The sword did not depart from his house, but God did not take the throne from him. **Divine correction does not eliminate pain, but it transforms it into maturity.** Many of the deepest psalms emerge from this period. David no longer sings only about victories, but about mercy—about how brokenness attracts divine favor. Discipline makes us more human and, paradoxically, more like God. It reminds us that we are dust, dependent on grace.

Just as Paul heard from Jesus:

> *"My grace is sufficient for you, for My strength is made perfect in weakness".*
>
> (2 Corinthians 12:9)

THE STORY DOES NOT END IN YOUR FAILURE

If David's life teaches us anything, it is that **failure does not have the final word.** After his fall, he wrote Psalm 51:

> *"Create in me a clean heart, O God, and renew a steadfast spirit within me".*
>
> (Psalm 51:10)

Did you notice that he does not simply ask, "forgive me"? He asks for a new heart. David understood that his problem was not just a single act, but an internal condition. God's grace does not merely cancel sin; it offers a transformed heart. And that renewed heart is expressed through action: David promises to teach transgressors. His failure becomes a platform for ministry. The wound becomes a weapon.

> *"And we know that all things work together for good to those who love God, to those who are the called according to His purpose".*
>
> (Romans 8:28)

That includes our own missteps. God is so sovereign that He not only redeems what others do to us, but also what we do voluntarily. What does this mean? That your worst mistake can be recycled by God into a story of grace. Not in the sense that He approves it, but in the sense that He can bring something beautiful out of what was ugly. Jesus' genealogy includes Bathsheba, called "the wife of Uriah." The evangelist Matthew does not omit her. Why? To show that the Messianic line runs through broken stories. That reminds me that my failures do not disqualify me from God's plan; they are opportunities for His grace to shine.

We must also remember that David was forgiven, but the sword did not depart from his house. The consequences remained. This teaches us that grace does not eliminate responsibility. There are marriages that are not restored, ministries that are paused, opportunities that are permanently lost. **Grace is not an eraser; it is redemption.** It is as if God were saying, "Even though what you did has no human remedy, I will write a new chapter over it." That new chapter does not mean forgetting what happened, but reinterpreting it. Healed wounds serve to keep others from repeating the same story. That is why we can say that our wounds become our weapons. Paul accepted his "thorn" because he knew that through it the power of Christ was revealed.

So why move forward?

> "If we confess our sins, He is faithful and just to forgive us our sins and to cleanse us from all unrighteousness".
>
> *(1 John 1:9)*

> "Through the LORD's mercies we are not consumed, because His compassions fail not. They are new every morning; great is Your faithfulness".
>
> *(Lamentations 3:22–23)*

These promises tell us that each day is a new opportunity. Grace writes a different ending. That does not minimize the damage, but it offers hope. The question is whether we will accept that grace—or remain trapped in regret.

GENERAL REFLECTIONS ON HUMAN FRAGILITY

Although I do not share my full personal story here, I know what it is like to struggle with sins that do not fit the cliché of "the devil made me do it." I know what it is to be a musician in a church and still battle secret temptations. I know the weight of voluntary sins and how shame tries to convince you that there is no way back. I also know that many live similar processes: people who served for years and, in a moment of weakness, fell. Some were exposed through confrontation, not confession. That creates painful dynamics: the offender feels unmasked, and the offended feels betrayed. In the end, everyone needs grace.

When I read about David, I am encouraged because his life is complex. He is not a perfect hero nor an irredeemable villain. He is a human being with virtues and weaknesses. That balance helps me accept my humanity. The Bible does not romanticize its characters; it presents them with all their contradictions. Neither does it cancel them when they fail. This teaches me to be merciful with myself and with others. At the same time, it reminds me that I cannot blame the enemy for things that spring from my own desires. Spiritual warfare is real, but personal responsibility is also real. I cannot justify myself by saying, "it was a battle"; in many cases, it was my choice.

If today you are in process—settling into a new church, seeking community, returning to tithing after a season—let me encourage you: **it is a step of faith.** The pastor may not yet know you by name, but God does. Every act of obedience is a seed. Even if your past story feels heavy, grace can write chapters of service and growth. This book does not have to tell everything right now. There will be time and space for more personal testimonies when God so indicates. In the meantime, we can speak of biblical truth, of human fragility, and of divine faithfulness.

Shame wants you silent; grace wants you standing.

THE QUESTION THAT REDEEMS

Let us return to Nathan's question: "Why have you despised the word of God?" That question still echoes today. The temptation is to blame circumstances or external forces. But honesty requires us to recognize that many times we despise the word by choice. We do not want to submit our desires to the divine will. We prefer the immediate over the eternal. Even so, God's question does not seek to condemn, but to redeem. It invites us to see the seriousness of our sin in order to appreciate the magnitude of His grace. It reminds us that although God forgives and restores, human beings still carry scars. And it calls us to walk in humility, knowing that our decisions affect those we love.

There are confessions made in public, and others that are whispered only in the presence of God. Not every wound needs to be exposed in order to be healed, but when our actions have hurt someone, confession becomes a doorway to restoration. Silence may seem easier, but prolonged silence deepens the pain. Speaking with humility, acknowledging the fault, and asking for forgiveness opens space for grace to heal what pride kept wounded. Sometimes forgiveness does not come immediately, but God honors every sincere step toward the truth. The Christian faith is not a spectacle of confessions, but an invitation to look inward, to allow the Holy Spirit to illuminate our shadows, and to restore what was broken with love and patience. David did not publish his sin in a public square; he confessed it to God and then wrote psalms born out of brokenness. There is a time to speak and a time to remain silent, and both can be acts of obedience. Today, what matters is understanding that God asks in order to rescue, that shame is a chain, that discipline is love, and that grace has the final word.

This chapter ends with an invitation: to let the word of God carry more weight than our emotions, to take responsibility for our weaknesses, and to embrace the grace that writes new endings. May we, like David, be able to say, "Create in me, O God, a clean heart," and may our brokenness not be the epitaph, but the prologue of a story of redemption.

Because in the end, grace does not only forgive your past—it also gives you back your future.

PRAYER

Lord, today I do not justify myself, nor do I hide.
I acknowledge the times I have taken Your word lightly
and the moments when I have preferred my desire over Your truth.

Thank You because Your grace does not cancel me—it corrects me.
Thank You because You do not reject the one who turns to You
with a sincere heart.

Teach me to live with a clean heart,
to take responsibility with humility,
and to walk in obedience without fear of my past.

May Your word carry more weight than my shame,
and may Your grace write what I cannot repair.

In the name of Jesus. Amen.

CHAPTER 7

WHAT ARE YOU DOING HERE?

Rejection that redirects

ELIJAH

BEFORE THE FIRE:
THE MAN WHO APPEARED SUDDENLY

Rejection is a central theme in the story of Elijah and in our own lives. God uses rejection not to destroy us, but to redirect us. This story teaches us that even when the fire goes out, God is still present.

Elijah's story begins without warning, without lineage, without visible preparation. There is no long introduction or genealogical record—he simply appears on the scene, as if heaven had sent him without prior notice.

> *"Then Elijah the Tishbite, of the inhabitants of Gilead, said to Ahab, 'As the LORD God of Israel lives, before whom I stand, there shall not be dew nor rain these years, except at my word.'"*
>
> *(1 Kings 17:1)*

Just like that, without advance notice, a man dares to stop the rain with a single word. No one knew him, but everyone knew his name after that moment. Elijah emerges during the reign of King Ahab and his wife, Queen Jezebel—two figures who had corrupted worship in Israel, filling the nation with idols and false prophets.

The people no longer knew who God was, and God raises up a prophet whose name means "My God is the LORD." The message was hidden in his identity. Every time they spoke his name, it was as if heaven reminded them: "The LORD is still God."

From the very first day, Elijah learned that obeying God is not always comfortable. After delivering the word of judgment, he had to hide by the Brook Cherith. There he was fed by ravens—unclean creatures, yet obedient. And when the brook dried up,

God sent him to a widow in Zarephath, a foreign woman with an empty pantry.

> *"And the LORD heard the voice of Elijah; and the soul of the child came back to him, and he revived".*
>
> *(1 Kings 17:22)*

Elijah witnessed how the oil and the flour did not run out, and how life returned to the body of a dead child. He saw the power of God in the hidden place before seeing it in public. God always forms His prophets far from applause. Before the fire on Mount Carmel, there is a quiet brook where dependence is learned. Before being a public voice, one must be a private listener.

His story teaches us that the strongest callings are born in small places. Elijah was not recruited by a temple or appointed by a king; he was raised up by divine necessity. And it was precisely that desert man, that solitary figure from Gilead, whom God used to reignite the faith of a nation.

WHEN THE FIRE GOES OUT

Elijah had seen what few eyes have ever seen: fire falling from heaven, an altar ignited without a human spark, the people shouting, "The LORD, He is God! The LORD, He is God!" In that moment, the prophet was not simply a servant—he was a living flame. God had backed his prayer with power, had shown who truly ruled over Israel, and Elijah had been the instrument. It was the kind of victory anyone would envy, the moment when one might think, "After this, everything will be glory."

But right after the fire... came the silence. And in that silence, the prophet who had confronted hundreds of false prophets began to flee from a single woman:

> *"And when he saw that, he arose and ran for his life, and went to Beersheba, which belongs to Judah, and left his servant there. But he himself went a day's journey into the wilderness, and came and sat down under a broom tree. And he prayed that he might die, and said, 'It is enough! Now, LORD, take my life, for I am no better than my fathers.'"*
>
> *(1 Kings 19:3–4)*

The man who had called down fire from heaven now only wanted to sleep under a tree. The same one who challenged false gods was now asking to die. And here we discover a truth that is often hard for us to accept: after the fire, there is also exhaustion; after success, there is also loneliness; after the noise, silence arrives—and not everyone knows what to do with it.

THE PROPHET WHO WANTED TO EXTINGUISH HIS CALLING

Elijah did not doubt the power of God, but he did doubt his place in the story. He had done everything right, yet nothing seemed to change. The people were still divided. The queen was still on her throne. And fear—that emotion he had overcome so many times—this time caught up with him. There is a difference between being tired and being empty. Tiredness is relieved by sleep, but emptiness is healed by listening to the right voice.

God did not interrupt his rest. He did not rebuke him for running away. He allowed him to sleep and fed him with bread and water. An angel touched him twice and said:

> *"Arise and eat, because the journey is too great for you".*
>
> *(1 Kings 19:7)*

There was no sermon, no reproach, no condemnation. Only bread, rest, and divine patience. Because before restoring a servant, God repairs the body and the soul. God did not rebuke him for fleeing; He fed him so he could return. For there are escapes that are part of the process, not signs of failure.

WHEN REJECTION FEELS LIKE FAILURE

Elijah did not run only because of fear. He ran because he felt rejected. Not by God, but by the people who should have changed and did not. Nothing hurts more than giving everything for others and seeing them remain the same. Nothing wounds the heart of a servant more than the feeling that his effort was useless.

> *"I have been very zealous for the LORD God of hosts; for the children of Israel have forsaken Your covenant, torn down Your altars, and killed Your prophets with the sword. I alone am left; and they seek to take my life".*
>
> *(1 Kings 19:10)*

These were not mere words... they were an emotional confession. Elijah was not lying; he was exhausted from being right in a world that did not want to listen. How many times rejection does not come from enemies, but from those we love most. How often the pain is not in open offense, but in indifference. Elijah had obeyed, but he felt alone, out of place, and forgotten. And when the soul feels rejected, the mind begins to create its own caves.

Rejection whispers in your ear and convinces you that your story is over.

WHAT SCIENCE CONFIRMS

Today, science has begun to put words to realities that the Bible has shown for centuries. Neuroscience has observed that social rejection is not only an emotional experience, but also a bodily one: the brain processes rejection in a way very similar to physical pain. In other words, rejection truly hurts. It is not exaggeration or weakness; it is a real biological response of the human being.

That is why, when rejection is prolonged, its impact does not remain only in feelings. It ends up showing in the body: persistent fatigue, anxiety, irritability, isolation, or silence. And among many men, shaped by a culture that taught them to "endure" and not show vulnerability, that pain is often camouflaged behind simple but deep phrases:

"I'm fine."
"It's nothing."
"I just need time."

But God does not ignore that pain. Elijah also came to say, "It is enough," and God did not accuse him of a lack of faith nor confront him harshly. He attended to him. He gave him rest, food, and presence.

Scripture says that an angel touched him and said:

"Arise and eat." (1 Kings 19:5)

Then he ate, drank, and lay down again, and in the strength of that food he walked forty days *(1 Kings 19:6–8)*. God treated his emotional exhaustion for what it was: an internal wound. The pain of rejection does not frighten God; it opens the door for Him to meet you from a deeper place.

WHEN GOD SEEKS YOU IN THE CAVE
Elijah walked forty days and forty nights to Horeb, the mountain of God. He was no longer running out of fear... he was running because he did not know where else to go. And when he arrived, he went into a cave. There, in the middle of his isolation, God did not forget him:

"What are you doing here, Elijah?" (1 Kings 19:9)

It was not a geographical question. It was a question of the soul. It was not, "Where are you?" but, "Why are you where I did not call you to be?" Elijah thought God had left him, but it was God who went looking for him. Because even though he had resigned from the calling, the calling had not resigned from him.

And here begins the most beautiful part of the process: God

does not take him back to Carmel, but leads him into a more intimate encounter. There is no longer fire falling, no crowds shouting, no enemies pursuing. Only silence. And in that silence, God teaches him something that every calling needs to learn:

"And after the fire, a still small voice". (1 Kings 19:12)

The power that once came with fire now arrives with calm. Elijah expected noise, but God chose to whisper.

> *When God lowers the volume, it is because He wants to speak to you more closely.*

KNOWING IT AND NOT DOING IT

Rejection does not frighten God; it gives Him the opportunity to find you again. Sometimes the greatest weight does not come from what we ignore, but from what we know and do not do. Elijah knew the voice of God. He had heard it so many times that he could distinguish it between the wind and the fire.

Yet even knowing, he ran. Because we do not always run from a lack of faith, but from an excess of weariness. "Knowing it and not doing it" is the point where knowledge does not become obedience, where the spirit wants to move forward, but the body sits down under the broom tree. And that point— I have seen it up close.

WHEN REJECTION COMES FROM WITHIN

There is a kind of rejection that does not come from the outside, but from within. It has no face and no name, yet it walks with you every morning when you wake up and asks, "What if it wasn't God who spoke to you?" It is that inner voice that makes you doubt what you were once sure of. The one that whispers, "You're moving too fast." "Maybe you should wait." What will others say? Will they laugh at you? And what if what God told you... wasn't God?

I have discovered that the worst rejection does not always come from the crowd, but from the mirror. Because there are moments when I am not afraid that others will close doors on me—I am afraid that I will close them myself. God gave me a clear calling: to write, to speak, to leave a message. But many times, before writing the first line, I am already fighting an invisible battle. I doubt whether the message is right, whether the timing is appropriate, whether people will receive it. And in that inner dialogue, I begin to reject what God had already affirmed. I ask myself, "Did I get ahead of myself?" or "Was it really God?" What was certainty one day becomes doubt the next.

It is a painful cycle. Because one part of me believes and another part hides. One part kneels in gratitude, and another kneels asking forgiveness for doubting. Every morning I begin the day with that double prayer: "Lord, forgive me if this is not what You have for me," and at the same time, "Forgive me because this is what You have for me and I have rejected it out of fear." I live between hope and fear, between confidence and indecision. And I know it is not healthy, but this is the struggle of self-rejection.

Only in prayer do I find peace. When I close my eyes and

speak with God, His Spirit redirects me and, with patience, reminds me of what He placed within me. I believe that many of the things God spoke to me in my youth were stalled by bad decisions, distractions, or by that same question: "Was it You, God?" I have held myself back out of fear of being rejected for being the one who brings the word. But despite my doubts, God has not given up on me. He continues to confirm His calling, even though I have questioned it a thousand times.

He does not grow tired of affirming me when I grow tired of believing.

GOD CAN BRING YOU OUT OF THIS

Sometimes we pray, "Lord, if You get me out of this, I will never do it again." And minutes later, we forget the promise. Because deliverance is not always dramatic. Sometimes it does not come with shouting, or tears, or fire from heaven. Sometimes it is simply getting up one more day, even though you feel like you failed yesterday.

I myself have been there. There were moments when I thought I had already overcome something—that God had completely delivered me from a certain struggle—and suddenly, I found myself once again walking close to what I thought was behind me. That discouraged me. I would think, "Lord, how is it possible that I am still battling this if You had already taken me out of it?" And God taught me that not every setback is a defeat; sometimes it is simply a way of reminding you where He brought you from. Freedom does not always look like an open door; sometimes it looks like a renewed mind. We all have places from which we once said, "I'm out of that," yet at some point we feel the pull to return. And still, the grace of God does not run out in our returns, because even when we turn back, God continues to wait for us with purpose.

REDIRECTION OF PURPOSE

Elijah's story does not end in the cave; it ends on the road. *"Then the LORD said to him: Go, return on your way..." (1 Kings 19:15).* God lifted him up, reminded him of his mission, and sent him back with a new assignment. Elijah thought his story was over, but God still had names to pronounce, kings to anoint, and generations to awaken. God's purpose is not canceled by exhaustion; it is redirected by compassion.

If Elijah had stayed in the cave, his successor Elisha would never have received the anointing. The day he found Elisha plowing with twelve yoke of oxen, Elijah threw his mantle over him *(1 Kings 19:19)*. That simple gesture began a chain of miracles in the next generation. Elisha, who received the mantle, performed double the miracles of his master. If Elijah had given in to rejection and weariness, Elisha would not have been called, the oil would not have multiplied in the widow's house, the axe head would not have floated on the water, and Naaman would not have been healed of leprosy. Elijah's faithfulness opened the way for someone else to go farther. God is not only thinking about your story; He is thinking about those who will come after you. If you stop, what impact will it have on them?

Sometimes the fire does not destroy you; it refines you. And I understood something: God does not only form prophets on Mount Carmel; He also forms hearts in caves. Many of us think the goal is to feel again what we once felt, but God does not want to take you backward; He wants to take you deeper. He is not looking for you to repeat your moment of fire, but to learn how to walk even when there is no fire.

Because if you have learned to obey in the fire and to listen in the silence, you are ready to keep walking without depending on emotions.

RESTARTING FROM THE CAVE

There are moments when the soul needs a restart—not because God has changed His plan, but because we have filled ourselves with too many open windows: thoughts, fears, external voices, and internal doubts. Like a computer that has been on for hours, processing too many tasks at once, the heart begins to overheat.

That is what happened to Elijah. He did not lose faith; he lost stability. His mind became saturated with images, threats, exhaustion, and guilt. God did not replace him; He restarted him.

When the angel said, "Arise and eat," it was like pressing restart. He was not a new prophet; he was the same one— restored. Elijah did not need a new mission; he needed to function again.

Sometimes we think we need a new calling, when what we really need is for the Holy Spirit to close the applications that are draining our faith. Fears running in the background, comparisons that consume energy, memories that keep occupying emotional memory—all of that slows the soul down.

And God, with patience, does what a loving technician would

do: He does not erase your hard drive; He restarts you with what still works. The same fire, the same word—but now with an updated heart.

When Elijah came out of the cave, he was not a different man; he was a restored man. And when you come out of yours, you will not be a stranger, but the best version of yourself—the version that remembers that its power is not in speed, but in obedience.

DELIVERANCE: NOT ALWAYS DRAMATIC

In many congregations, deliverance is spoken of as an instant act—something that happens at an altar with shouting and tears. And while that can happen, it is not the only way God delivers. Sometimes deliverance is a silent process, almost imperceptible, like the dawn. It begins with a new thought, a daily decision, a chain that slowly loosens.

I have prayed those prayers: "If You get me out of this, I will never fall again." And yet, minutes later, I was the same. God does not give up; neither does He mock us. He understands that our flesh is weak. Deliverance is sometimes a walk; other times, a run. But what matters is that He walks beside us. Every small step, every victory over an impulse, is a celebration in heaven.

TOOLS FOR EMBRACING REJECTION

- **Take it to God in prayer.** No feeling is too small for His attention. Tell Him how it hurts, how it frustrated you, and how it made you doubt yourself. Honesty is the doorway to healing.

- **Seek community.** Elijah thought he was alone, but God told him there were seven thousand who had not bowed the knee to Baal. In the body of Christ, there is always someone who understands your process. We do not walk alone.

- **Serve others.** Few things heal like focusing our energy on blessing others. When you help, comfort, and serve, your perspective shifts. You discover that your life has purpose, even when others have rejected you. Your service to others may be God's answer to your own wound.

REFLECTION EXERCISES

- Take a few minutes to think about the times you have been rejected. What did that experience teach you? How did it shape you? Write it down. Rereading your story will help you see God's hand in every chapter.

- Think about an area in which you swore you would never fail again, yet you still do. Write down one small action you can take today. Remember that change happens step by step.

- Finally, reflect on the story of Elijah. In which moments did you identify with him? Where do you recognize God searching for you in your cave? Allow His gentle voice to redirect you.

WHAT ARE YOU DOING HERE?

As I mentioned at the beginning, when God asked Elijah, "What are you doing here?", it was not a geographical question. It was a question of the soul. He was not saying,

"Where are you?", but "Why did you stop?" That question still resonates today.

What are you doing here?

How many times have you asked God to use you and, at the first rejection, you stopped?

How many times, after crying out for purpose, did you stop acting when you heard a "no"?

How many times have you buried what God gave you because someone did not value it or because you yourself despised it?

This is not about going against the direction of your leader or your family, but about not extinguishing what God ignited out of fear of others' opinions or the inner voice that says, "Maybe it wasn't God." Seek the guidance of the Holy Spirit, but do not use doubt as an excuse to stay in the cave.

Think about specific moments in your life when God has asked you this question. Maybe it was when you shared a dream and someone mocked it. Maybe it was when you posted a message and no one reacted. Maybe it was when you presented an idea and were rejected. In those moments, God whispers to you: "What are you doing here? Why did you stop moving forward?" The question does not come to condemn you, but to invite you to keep going.

And I understood that grace is not only what forgives you, but also what lifts you up. God does not seek you to judge you, but to remind you who you are. Many times we pray, "God, use me; I am willing to do anything, to do Your will," and at the first rejection we pause. It is time to step out and act regardless of what others say, even when rejection comes from within or from a leader. This is not about ignoring authority; it is about obeying the Spirit of God. Do not self-sabotage the calling or the message He gave you. Your story does not end in the cave.

Rejection is not the end; it is the beginning of a new chapter. Get up, eat, and keep going—there is still a long journey ahead.

> *"And behold, the word of the LORD came to him, and He said to him, 'What are you doing here, Elijah?'"*
>
> *(1 Kings 19:9)*

PRAYER

Lord, today I bring before You everything I have carried in silence: the words that wounded me, the "no's" that dimmed my fire, the doors that closed when I thought they would open, and the caves where I hid, believing it was the end.

You know every corner where my soul said, "Enough." You know my fears, my doubts, and that deep weariness that cannot be cured by sleep, but by hearing Your voice.

Today I hear Your question:
"What are you doing here?"
Not as judgment, but as a calling.
Not as reproach, but as an invitation.
That question reveals that You never left me alone,
that even when I hid, You came looking for me.

Lord, heal in me the weight of rejection.
Uproot the lies I told myself,
the doubts I raised like walls,
and the inner voice that made me believe I was not enough.
Close the invisible wounds that stopped me,
and restore the confidence that fear stole from me.

Allow me to hear Your gentle whisper.
Speak to me in the silence, when the fire is gone,

when there is no applause, when everything seems still.
Teach me to recognize You there as well,
where no one sees me, where only You find me.

Redirect me, Lord.
Restart my heart.
Restore my strength.
Give me back the vision that grew dim in the cave,
and renew the calling that I myself tried to extinguish.

Today I choose to rise, even if slowly.
I take the bread and the water You give me.
I set my feet on the path once again,
not because I am strong,
but because You go with me
and because a long journey still lies ahead.

In the name of Jesus. Amen.

CHAPTER 8
WHO TOUCHED ME?

I Am Not Who I Thought I Was: When Jesus Redefines Your Identity

THE WOMAN WITH
THE FLOW OF BLOOD

THE DAY THE QUESTION FOUND ME

Sometimes we write without realizing that, between line and line, God is touching the soul. This chapter found me that way: with an open heart, with memories that still hurt, with wounds I thought were no longer bleeding.

As I wrote it, I felt that it was not I who was pursuing the story, but the story that was coming to find me.

And I thought:

How many times have I approached Jesus just like this woman? Quiet, timid, broken, not wanting to disturb anyone, yet desperately needing a touch.

Maybe that is why I cried when I read it again. Because I understood that this question—"Who touched Me?"—was not only for her.

It was also for me. And perhaps... it is for you too.

THE QUESTION THAT STOPS
THE ONE WHO NEVER STOPS

There are questions that sound like a rebuke, and others that sound like an embrace. *"Who touched Me?"* sounds like both.

The scene is holy chaos. Jesus is walking toward Jairus's house, an important man with an urgent problem: his daughter is dying. This is not a routine visit, not a pastoral call with coffee and cookies.

It is a race against time. The crowd presses in on Him— everyone pushes Him, everyone pulls at Him, everyone wants something. Jesus seems unstoppable... until He stops.

In the middle of the pushing, the sweat, the shouting of the people, the Master suddenly comes to a halt and asks a question no one understands: "Who touched Me?"

The disciples look at Him the way people look at a pastor when he asks a strange question in the middle of a service:

"Lord… everyone is touching You. What kind of question is that?"

But Jesus knows the difference. One thing is to brush against Him by accident; another is to touch Him with intention. One thing is to be near Him out of habit; another is to reach for Him out of desperation. One thing is to be part of the crowd; another is to respond to the call.

This chapter is not only about a sick woman. It is about a calling hidden inside a crisis. It is about the voice of Jesus asking in the middle of the noise, "Who touched Me?" and waiting for someone—amid guilt, shame, and exhaustion—to dare to say, "It was me, Lord."

Because the call of God often begins this way: with a timid touch and a question that forces you to step out of anonymity.

TWO STORIES, THE SAME CLOCK

Mark 5 presents two stories running in parallel, like two clocks marking the same hour with different hands. On one side, Jairus: a synagogue leader, an important name, a respected position, a sick daughter, a public problem. On the other, a woman with no name, no title, no position—also with a public problem, but one hidden away.

Twelve years of illness for her.
Twelve years of life for Jairus's daughter.

While one life was growing, the other was fading. While a little girl was learning to walk, a woman was learning to hide. While birthdays were celebrated in one house, years of shame were counted in another.

God is an expert at synchronizing stories we believe have nothing to do with each other. What looks like coincidence to us is choreography to Him. A respected leader and a marginalized woman, an anguished father and a forgotten daughter—all end up meeting on the same road, with the same Jesus, under the same question: "Who touched Me?"

And here the theme of this book begins to emerge: **the call.**

Because Jairus knew his position, but that afternoon he discovered his true posture: a desperate father at the feet of Jesus. The woman knew her problem, but that afternoon she discovered her true identity: a beloved daughter, called by her name.

The call of God has that habit: it knocks one person down from a pedestal and lifts another up from the ground, bringing both to the same place—to the feet of the Master.

THE WOMAN WITHOUT A NAME AND THE CRUELEST NICKNAME

The Gospels do not tell us her name. We do not know if she was called Rachel, Mary, Deborah, Carmen, or Luisa. In heaven we will know; here we only know her nickname: "the woman with the flow of blood," "the woman with the issue of blood."

How cruel it is when your identity becomes permanently attached to your problem.

She is not remembered for her dreams, her character, her childhood smile, or the song she loved when she was young. She is remembered for her hemorrhage.

In our churches and families, we also use nicknames disguised as "descriptions":

- "The one with the bad temper"

- "The divorced one"

- "The pastor's child who fell"

- "The one who walked away"

- "The addict"

- "The one with the troubled children"

And little by little, if we are not careful, we begin to believe that we are our nickname. We do not say, "I have a struggle"; we say, "This is just how I am." We do not say, "I am going through this"; we say, "This is who I am."

The woman with the issue of blood was much more than her illness, but twelve years are enough to convince you that your pain is your definition. Twelve years are enough for people to stop calling you by your name and start calling you by your wound.

Hear this from now on:
Your calling does not begin with your nickname; it begins with
the voice of Jesus breaking that nickname.

BLEEDING ON THE INSIDE:
WHEN NO ONE SEES WHERE YOU ARE DYING

What made her situation even more painful was that her bleeding was internal. It was not a visible wound on her forehead, nor a cast on her arm, nor a limp in her walk. It was a hemorrhage in the most intimate part of her body, in a place no one sees, no one comments on, no one wants to mention.

If she had arrived bleeding from the nose, someone would have handed her a tissue.

If she had a wound on her forehead, someone would have taken her to the doctor.

But she was bleeding in secret.

And that is where many of us are today. There is no cast on the soul, no bandage on the heart, no emotional crutches that others can easily notice. These are bleedings hidden behind a smile at church, behind a well-rehearsed "I'm fine, I'm walking in victory."

You bleed on the inside when:

- You have professional success, but no peace in your bed or on your pillow.

- You serve in church, but you get home feeling empty, used, drained.

- You post happy pictures on social media, but you do not want to talk to anyone off the screen.

- You are the funny one in the group, but at night you are the loneliest of all.

People see your posts, your clothes, your car, your ministry—but they do not see where you bleed. They do not see the area of your life where you feel less than, dirty, unworthy, exhausted.

The woman with the issue of blood represents all of us who are "functioning" on the outside, but losing life on the inside.

And here is the detail: God's calling does not ignore those bleedings. God does not call only the strong; He calls those who feel they have no blood left to lose. He does not call only those who are "whole"; He calls those who feel empty, used, worn out.

DOCTORS, REMEDIES, AND SOLUTIONS THAT ONLY MAKE IT WORSE

Mark tells us that she "had suffered many things from many physicians. She had spent all that she had and was no better, but rather grew worse." She was not only sick; she was also in debt, exhausted, and disappointed.

She tried everything:

- The trending remedy of the moment

- The neighbor's advice

- The doctor recommended in the WhatsApp group

- The "cure-all" from the advertisement

Nothing worked. In fact, she got worse.

The same thing happens to us. To cover the inner bleeding, we try everything: overworking, distractions, toxic relationships, endless entertainment, food, shopping, ministry without rest. For a moment it seems to work, but in the end we are left emptier than before.

What hurts the most is when we also try "spiritual methods" out of habit: we go to church without heart, we serve without communion, we repeat verses without faith—all trying to calm the hemorrhage of the soul with religious band-aids.

Until, like this woman, we realize that we are spending everything we have and, instead of getting better, we are getting worse.

Maybe you are there. You feel called by God, but you do not feel whole enough to respond. You sense that God wants to use you, but all you can think is, "Lord, I am bleeding too much to talk about calling."

And yet, it is precisely there that the calling begins to take shape.

THE HIDDEN PROCESS OF THE MIRACLE: HEARD, CAME, THOUGHT, TOUCHED

The Bible gives us four verbs that become a spiritual map of calling:

"When she heard about Jesus, she came behind Him in the crowd and touched His garment. For she said, 'If only I may touch His clothes, I shall be made well.'"

(Mark 5:27–28)

1. Heard.

2. Came.

3. Thought (she said within herself).

4. Touched.

Sometimes we preach the touch, but we forget everything that happened before it.

First, **she heard.** Someone spoke to her about Jesus. We do not know who. It may have been a neighbor, a family member, a street vendor. Someone told her, "That Rabbi heals. That Rabbi does not reject. That Rabbi touches the unclean."

This is how almost every calling begins: with someone speaking to you about Jesus in a way that awakens something inside you. It is not just information; it is invitation. It is not only a biblical fact; it is a seed of faith.

Then, **she came.** Hearing the story was not enough. She could have said, "How beautiful what God does for others," and stayed home. But she got up, got dressed, covered herself as best she could, and pushed her way into the crowd.

Calling always pulls you out of comfort. It makes you rise from your usual spiritual place. It leads you to cross spaces where you do not feel worthy. It pushes you to walk toward places where you are not sure you will be welcomed.

After that, **she thought.** "She said within herself...". That inner monologue, that conversation inside the mind, is often the true battlefield of calling. On one side, the voice that says, "Why go? Nothing will change. You are not worthy. You are not enough." On the other, a new voice—small but persistent: "If I only touch Him... something can happen."

God's calling always fights first in your thoughts before it manifests in your actions. That is why the enemy attacks your mind: he wants to convince you that it makes no sense to try, that it is too late, that you have tried too much already, that God has forgotten you.

And finally, **she touched.** That touch was not elegant or liturgical. It did not have the form of a perfect prayer. It did not follow the protocol of a well-structured service. It was a desperate act of faith—a "please, excuse me," a timid push through the elbows of the crowd: "Let me pass, even if I have to crouch, even if I have to be on my knees, even if I can only reach the edge of His garment."

If you want to respond to God's calling, the order does not change:

You hear. You come. You think differently. You dare to touch.

> *Do not wait to feel perfect to touch Him. Do not wait for the bleeding to stop before you draw near. It is the touch of faith that stops the hemorrhage—not the other way around.*

The Miracle in the Body and the Miracle Along the Way

"And immediately the fountain of her blood was dried up, and she felt in her body that she was healed of the affliction".

(Mark 5:29)

In an instant, twelve years of bleeding stopped. Twelve years of shame, odor, discomfort, stained clothing, purification rituals—all ended with a single touch.

Meanwhile, Jesus was on His way to Jairus's house. From Jairus's perspective, this woman was an obstacle, an interruption, a dangerous delay. From Jesus' perspective, she was a divine appointment—part of the plan, a necessary stop.

Here is something vitally important for calling: many of the miracles that mark your life will not happen where you thought God was going to do "the big thing," but right in the middle of the journey toward something else that seemed more important.

Maybe you wanted God to do a great miracle in your ministry, and He decides to begin by doing it in your living room, your kitchen, your workplace. Maybe you thought your calling would be seen from a pulpit, and God decides to begin on that dark day when you simply dared to say, "Lord, help me," and you touched His garment through tears.

Jesus is not bothered by the interruption. We are. We watch the clock, complain about the delay, get angry at the traffic. He sees people. He sees daughters. He sees sons.

He sees callings hidden in the crowd.

"WHO TOUCHED ME?" — THE QUESTION THAT REVEALS, NOT INVESTIGATES

"And Jesus, immediately knowing in Himself that power had gone out of Him, turned around in the crowd and said, 'Who touched My clothes?'"

(Mark 5:30)

Jesus knew that power had gone out from Him. He was not confused. He did not lose track. The battery of the Holy Spirit did not run low. He did not ask because He lacked information; He asked because He wanted to give someone identity.

Calling is always accompanied by questions from God that seem illogical:

- "Adam, where are you?" (as if He did not know)

- "Elijah, what are you doing here?"

- "Moses, what do you have in your hand?"

- "Gideon, have I not sent you?"

- "Why are you like this, Jonah?"

- "Why did you doubt, Peter?"

- And here: "Who touched Me?"

God does not ask questions to inform Himself; He asks them to transform us. He does not ask where you are to locate Himself, but to locate you.

He does not ask "Who touched Me?" to find out, but to give

154

the opportunity to confess, to come into the light, to stop hiding.

The woman could have remained silent. She could have slipped away into the crowd, happy with her physical miracle, but without confronting her shame. She had touched Jesus in secret, and now Jesus invites her to confess it in public.

Here fear and calling collide. Because responding to God's call almost always involves this: stopping the hiding of the places where you were healed. Stopping the pretense that you were never broken. Stopping the performance of a perfect church life to dare to say, "I bled there, I failed there, I suffered there—and there Jesus touched me."

"Who touched Me?" is a calling question.

It is Jesus saying, "I do not only want to change your condition; I want to change your story. I do not only want to stop your bleeding; I want to use your testimony."

THE SHAME THAT TREMBLES...
AND THE TRUTH THAT SETS FREE

> *"Then the woman, fearing and trembling, knowing what had happened to her, came and fell down before Him and told Him the whole truth".*
>
> (Mark 5:33)

I love that phrase: **"the whole truth."**

She did not give Him an edited testimony for social media.

She did not offer a short version "so as not to give a bad impression." She did not dress up her story to make it sound less ugly. She told Him everything.

We can imagine the scene: the crowd watching, Jairus checking the time, the disciples confused, and her—crying, trembling, telling it all:

- "I have been like this for twelve years…"

- "I spent everything I had…"

- "I feel unclean, rejected, powerless…"

- "Today I came afraid, hiding, thinking I would just touch You and run away…"

- "But when I touched You, I felt something I had never felt before…"

Daring to tell **"the whole truth"** is also part of the calling.

Because God does not call masks; He calls real people.
He does not anoint characters; He anoints testimonies.

Many of us are waiting for God to use us, but without releasing **"the whole truth."** We want a clean calling—without an embarrassing past, without a complicated story, without wounds. And Jesus insists on the opposite:

"Bring Me your complete truth. Not the edited version—the real one. I am not scandalized. I call you from right there."

THE NAME CHANGE: FROM "THE WOMAN WITH THE ISSUE" TO "DAUGHTER"

"And He said to her, Daughter, your faith has made you well. Go in peace, and be healed of your affliction".

(Mark 5:34)

Here is the heart of the chapter.

Jesus does not begin by saying "woman."
He does not call her "unclean."
He does not say "the one with the problem."

He calls her something no one had called her in twelve years: "Daughter."

This is the only moment in the Gospels where Jesus uses "daughter" in this deeply personal way. While He is on His way to heal Jairus's daughter, He stops to remind this woman that she, too, is a daughter.

That word—Daughter—is her true calling.

Before any ministry.
Before any service.
Before any title.
Before any church role.
Before any microphone.

That word comes first: daughter (or son).

You are not "the one who sings."
You are not "the preacher."
You are not "the intercessor."
You are not "the prophet."

Those are functions.
Your calling begins with **identity:** daughter, son.

Jesus does not want you to leave with a miracle but without carrying Heaven's last name. He does not want you to stop bleeding and still think like a beggar. He does not want you to receive healing and still see yourself as "the one with the problem."

That is why He calls her.
That is why He exposes her.
That is why He pulls her out of the crowd.

So she would not leave as a thief of a miracle,
but as a daughter reconciled with her Father.

Your calling does not begin when you step onto a platform;
it begins when you hear Jesus whisper to you:

*"**Daughter... Son...** your faith has saved you.".*

WHAT DOES THIS HAVE TO DO WITH THE CALLING... AND WITH YOU?

You might be wondering:

"What does all of this have to do with calling? This story seems more about healing than ministry."

That is exactly the point.

Many of us want to discover what God wants us to do without first allowing Him to touch who we are on the inside. We want the map of ministry without passing through the hospital of the heart. We want the plan without the process.

The woman with the issue of blood teaches us that:
- Before she was sent, she was healed.

- Before she was used, she was called "daughter."

- Before she could speak to others, she had to tell "the whole truth" before Jesus.

Your calling is not a way to compensate for your bleeding; it is not your way of proving your worth. Calling is God's response to your **identity in Him**, not to your **performance for Him.**

God does not call you so that you stop bleeding; He calls you **from the place where you bled,** and He transforms that place into testimony.

Maybe your calling will be to walk with others who bleed in the same place where you once bled.

Maybe it will be to accompany those who feel unclean, those who hide in the crowd, those who believe their only option is to "touch and run."

Maybe your calling is simply to look someone in the eyes and say:

"You are a daughter.

You are a son.

You are not your problem."

That is how calling is born—not from strength, but from healing; not from perfection, but from identity restored.

A TOUCH WITH A NAME AND A SURNAME

Let's return to Jesus' question: "Who touched Me?"

- He did not say, "Who brushed against Me?"

- He did not say, "Who pushed Me?"

- He did not say, "Who came close to Me?"

He said, **"Who touched Me?"**

As if that touch had a name and a story attached to it.

In the crowd, everyone was close to Jesus—but not everyone was connected to Him. There was a lot of physical proximity and very little active faith. A lot of noise, a lot of movement, a lot of hands—yet only one hand truly believed.

The same thing happens in our churches, gatherings, and events. We can be surrounded by Bibles, worship, sermons, conferences—and still never truly touch Him. We can know all the songs, all the verses, all the gestures, and still be bleeding in secret.

Before God's calling ever becomes something spectacular, **it is this: giving Jesus a touch with your name on it.**

Not the touch of "one more person in the crowd," but the touch of someone who dares to say, "Lord, this is between You and me. I don't know how—but if I touch You, something will change."

That touch might be:

- The honest prayer you finally pray without a mask.

- The yes you give when He asks you to forgive someone.

- The decision to obey in something small that no one else sees.

- The confession you make in time—before sin destroys you.

When you respond like that, Jesus still stops in the middle of everything and asks, "Who touched Me?"

Not because He doesn't know—but because He wants you to know that He noticed, and that this moment is part of your calling.

We are the crowd that presses in.

We are the disciples who sometimes don't understand Jesus' urgency for one single person.

We are Jairus—knowing God is powerful, yet confused as to why He would stop right now.

And we are the woman—trying to touch Him and slip away unnoticed.

God is not threatened by our mess or our misunderstandings.

He is so patient that, in the middle of human chaos, He pauses for one life, heals one body, and restores one identity.

Many of us want to serve God like Jairus:
"Lord, come to my house—use my position—let's do something big."

But we don't want to admit that we are also the woman:
"Lord, I'm bleeding on the inside, and I don't know who to tell."

A complete calling embraces both.

WHEN YOUR STORY BECOMES AN ANSWER TO SOMEONE ELSE'S CALLING

After this encounter, the Bible does not tell us what the woman did next. We don't know if she became a preacher, if she served in a church, or if she followed Jesus on His later journeys. That biblical silence is not accidental—it is beautiful.

What we do know is that she left with something she did not have before: identity.
She did not leave as "the woman with the issue of blood," but as a Daughter.

And a daughter who has been restored carries that restoration into every place she walks—without needing pulpits or platforms. Her walk becomes a message. Her gaze changes. The way she listens changes. Her compassion changes.
Imagine her returning to her community: the same streets, the

same people, the same looks—but she is no longer the same. She no longer walks bent under shame, but lifted by the voice of Jesus.

Because when Jesus restores you, you become a living reminder that He still stops for the forgotten, that He still feels timid touches, that He still changes names, that He still says:

"I know who you are... and you are Mine."

You don't need a microphone for that.

Sometimes all it takes is an honest conversation, a sincere embrace, a prayer spoken through tears, a gesture that flows from the heart of someone who has first been touched by Him.

Your story—just as it is, without embellishment—is evidence that Jesus still walks through the crowd, and that anyone who dares to touch Him, even from the ground, can rise hearing their true identity spoken aloud:
Daughter. Son. Loved. Seen. Restored.

APPLYING THIS TO OUR EVERYDAY LIFE

How do we bring all of this down to the everyday—to work, family, church, traffic, the grocery store line?

1. **Acknowledge where you are bleeding.** Don't deny it. Don't spiritualize your bleeding. Don't cover it up with phrases like "that's just how I am" or "that's in the past." If there are areas where you still lose your peace, your

courage, or your confidence, there is still a hemorrhage there. Don't be afraid to bring it to Jesus.

2. **Listen again to the story of Jesus.** Not just about religion, not just about church, not just about doctrine... but about Jesus. Return to the gospel. Read the stories where He touches the unclean, embraces children, weeps, and stops. Let the good news of who He is refresh your faith as if it were the first time.

3. **Dare to take a step toward Him.** Maybe you can't change everything at once, but you can take one step: pray again, return to the Word, seek counsel, reconcile with someone. Even a small step is a "coming" toward Him.

4. **Guard your thoughts.** The woman said, "If I only touch Him..." What are you saying on the inside? If your inner dialogue is "I'm not worthy," "I can't," "God is finished with me," that dialogue sabotages your calling. Ask the Holy Spirit to renew your mind so you can say, "If I seek Him, He will answer; if I touch Him, something will change."

5. **Touch Him with intention.** Don't settle into spiritual routine. When you sing, touch Him. When you hear the Word, touch Him. When you serve, touch Him. When you are alone in your room, touch Him. Not with perfect hands, but with sincere ones.

6. Respond when He asks, "Who touched Me?" There will be moments when you feel God lovingly exposing you, calling you forward, placing you in a situation where you must admit, "It was me, Lord. I was the one who needed this touch." Don't run. That exposure is part of your healing and your calling.

7. **Embrace your new name.** The world may know you by your past, your mistake, or your failure. Jesus calls you daughter, son. Practice that name. Remind yourself of it. Before you leave the house, say it out loud:

"I am a daughter. I am a son. I am not my mistake, not my record, not my hemorrhage. I am loved."

Because your calling doesn't begin with what you do—it begins with who you are when He names you.

A CALLING FOR THOSE WHO FEEL LIKE AN INTERRUPTION

I want to speak here to those who feel like they are an interruption in God's agenda. To those who think, "God has more important things to do than to attend to me. There are people worse off than I am, there are wars, there are global problems. Why would He stop for me?"

The woman with the issue of blood could have thought exactly that. Jesus was on His way to save a dying child. Humanly speaking, that seems more urgent, doesn't it? And yet—Jesus stopped.

If you feel that way—as a burden, just another number, another case in the endless line of problems—listen carefully:

Jesus is not like us. He does not look at the clock and say, "I don't have time." He does not prioritize based on social status or human importance. He stops for callings that no one else sees.

Maybe you yourself have learned to see yourself as an interruption in other people's lives:

"I ruin their day with my problems."

"I'm a burden."

"It's better if I don't say anything."

Jesus looks at you in the crowd, feels the touch of your faith, and does exactly what He did with that woman: He stops, looks around, and asks, "Who touched Me?"—because He wants you to know that to Him, you are not an interruption; you are an appointment.

Your calling may be born precisely there: in discovering that God stops for you. In that moment when you dare to believe that your story—no matter how broken—is important to Him.

AN ENDING THAT REMAINS OPEN: FROM THE FLOOR TO HIS FEET

The woman came to her encounter with Jesus almost crawling—hiding, trying not to be seen. She left walking upright, with the word "daughter" echoing in her heart.

The question "Who touched Me?" hovered in the air of that crowd, but it also continues to echo through every generation. Jesus still asks it today—not to point out the guilty, but to embrace the child.

This chapter does not want you to finish by admiring a brave woman from a distance. It wants to bring you to the same floor where she crawled, into the same crowd she slipped through, to the same edge of the garment she touched, and to the same place where Jesus called her "daughter."

Perhaps you have been serving God for years while bleeding in secret.

Perhaps you have been running from your calling because you feel unworthy.

Perhaps this very book has confronted you with questions from God that have made you uncomfortable.

In the middle of all that, Jesus looks at you and asks again: **"Who touched Me?"**

It is your opportunity to say:

"Lord, it was me. I need You. I have been bleeding in silence. I have spent everything trying to fix myself. I want to stop hiding. Take me from the nickname to identity, from shame to calling, from the crowd to Your feet."

And when you do, you will hear the same answer she heard:

"Daughter, son… your faith has made you well. Go in peace. Be healed of your affliction."

I do not know what form your calling will take after this. Maybe it will continue in the same church, the same job, with the same children, in the same house. But one thing I do know: you will no longer be "the one with the wound" or "the one with the problem." You will be the son, the daughter, who learned to touch Jesus in the middle of the crowd and to live as someone who was called by name.

Because in the end, your true identity is not "the one who was bleeding." Your true identity is the one Jesus spoke that day, when He stopped everything to look at you:

Daughter. Son. Called. Loved. Seen. Heard.

And that voice—stronger than any nickname—is the one that will cause this chapter not only to be read, but to be lived as part of God's calling over your life.

PRAYER

Lord Jesus, today I come to You without masks and with the whole truth.

Touch me where I am bleeding on the inside and call me by my name.

Remind me that I am Your son, Your daughter, and teach me to live in peace. Amen.

CHAPTER 9

WHY DID YOU DOUBT?

Let Go—or You Will Sink

PETER

THE MOMENT BETWEEN
"COME" AND "I AM SINKING"

"Why did you doubt?" This question Jesus asks Peter, in the middle of a storm, does not come as a rebuke, but as an invitation. It does not seek information; it reveals where our gaze was lost. "Why did you doubt?" is not a shout of anger; it is the voice of the Master holding the disciple while lifting him out of the water.

Sometimes we read the passage about walking on water as if it were an isolated story: a heroic moment followed by a failure. The account is found in Matthew 14:22–33, where we are told that, in the middle of the storm, Peter said to Jesus: *"Lord, if it is You, command me to come to You on the water"* *(Matthew 14:28).* And Jesus responded with a single word: *"Come."* But when we look closely—comma by comma—we discover that this is not just the story of a miracle. It is the story of a heart that wants to believe, that dares to step out of the boat, that wavers, that sinks, and yet is still held by Jesus. It is not a spectacle to admire, but a revelation to imitate: all of us have felt the wind against us, all of us have known fear and doubt. In the end, we will not remember only what Peter did, but what God can do through our doubts.

This chapter will not leave you watching the storm from a distance. It will take you into the boat, let you feel the wind, hear the roar of the waves, and walk with Peter in every hesitant step, every heartbeat, every desperate cry, and every moment when the hand of Jesus never fails. This is the story of "Why did you doubt?" but it is also the story of "Let go—or you will sink."

A Day of Miracles and a Night of Wind

Before the storm began, the disciples had witnessed a display of divine generosity. Jesus took five loaves and two fish, blessed them, and fed a multitude. They did not only see a miracle; they participated in it by distributing the bread and gathering the leftovers. Their faith rose as they saw supernatural provision—what could possibly threaten men who had just lived through something like that?

That miracle was part of a continuous sequence. They had seen the Master heal the sick, give sight to the blind, and set the oppressed free. They walked with a rabbi who taught with authority and transformed lives. They had witnessed Him raise Jairus's daughter and seen a woman healed by touching the edge of His garment. They were living "days of heaven on earth." That is why, after such a glorious day, it feels dramatic that Jesus ordered them to get into a boat and go to the other side. Moving from distributing miracles to rowing against the wind was going to test whether their faith was more than emotion.

The Gospels say that Jesus *made* His disciples get into the boat. It was not a suggestion. He compelled them to leave without Him while He dismissed the crowd. He did not explain why or give them a strategy for the crossing. He simply sent them. They obeyed, perhaps thinking He would catch up with them later. Obedience required them to leave the place of the miracle and enter a scene where there would be no crowds or applause—only darkness and water.

As they rowed, the night grew darker and the wind battered the boat. The Sea of Galilee, set in a valley, is prone to sudden storms. The disciples—some of them experienced fishermen—began to struggle against the waves. Physical exhaustion, lack of light, and the roar of the wind created an atmosphere of distress. Though they had just come from an impressive miracle, they were now soaked and fighting to move forward. The mix of weariness and fear began to erode their recent joy. This is how life often works: we move from "spiritual ecstasy" into an unexpected struggle.

This was not the first storm they had faced with Jesus. On another occasion, on the same lake, a tempest arose while Jesus slept in the stern. Terrified, they woke Him, crying out, "Lord, save us—we are perishing!" He got up, rebuked the wind and the sea, and there was a great calm. Then He asked them, "Why are you afraid? Where is your faith?" They learned that the Son of God has authority over nature and that, even when He seems indifferent, He is fully aware of their need. His question became a reminder: fear rises when we forget who is in the boat.

This time, the situation was different. The storm was similar, but Jesus was not visibly with them. In the previous storm, His physical presence—even while asleep—was comforting. Now they were alone, rowing against the wind with no Savior in sight. Feeling abandoned after having been sent by Jesus must have been confusing. Perhaps they wondered why He had forced them to leave; perhaps the temptation to resentment crept in: "Does He even care about us?" Emotions can distort memory. We can forget what God did just hours ago and feel betrayed by a temporary silence. Jesus' absence from the boat tested the quality of their faith: would they stand on what they knew of His character, or be driven by what they felt?

PETER: IMPULSIVE, HUMAN, CHOSEN

The figure of Simon Peter is fascinating. He was a fisherman from Galilee, a hard-working man accustomed to waves and wind. *"Now as Jesus was walking by the Sea of Galilee, He saw two brothers... casting a net into the sea, for they were fishermen"* *(Matthew 4:18).* When Jesus called him, he immediately left his nets and became one of the disciples closest to the Master: *"And they immediately left their nets and followed Him"* *(Matthew 4:20).*

The Bible presents him as passionate, impulsive, and brave; he spoke first and thought later. He was able to declare with conviction, *"You are the Christ, the Son of the living God"* *(Matthew 16:16),* and just a few verses later, when Jesus spoke about the cross, Peter rebuked Him, saying, *"Far be it from You, Lord; this shall not happen to You!"* *(Matthew 16:22).*

He promised absolute loyalty, even unto death:

> *"Even if all are made to stumble because of You, I will never be made to stumble".*
>
> *(Matthew 26:33)*

Yet only a few hours later, confronted by a servant girl and strangers, he denied knowing Jesus three times, until *"he went out and wept bitterly"* *(Matthew 26:75).*

In the Garden of Gethsemane, driven by his impetuous nature, he drew a sword to defend the Master: *"Then Simon Peter, having a sword, drew it and struck the high priest's servant"* *(John 18:10),* still not understanding that Jesus was surrendering willingly.

His bold temperament led him to mistakes, but his sincere love for Jesus was undeniable. This mixture of courage and clumsiness makes him relatable. Peter is not an idealized hero, but a deeply human disciple. And that is why his story reflects us: our sincere promises, our impulsive reactions, and our falls... and yet, the calling that God does not revoke.

After the resurrection, Peter experienced a profound transformation. The rooster that crowed after his denial was etched into his memory as a symbol of failure, but also as the beginning of restoring grace. The same Master who had once said to him, "Get behind Me, Satan!" now sought him tenderly on the shore.

There, by the burning coals, Jesus did not confront him with a sermon, but with questions. Not to humiliate him, but to heal him.

First, He called him by his old name, as if taking him back to the beginning, before the impulsive promises:

"Simon, son of Jonah, do you love Me more than these?"

(John 21:15)

Peter responded without promising more than he could sustain:

"Yes, Lord; You know that I love You."

Then Jesus said to him:
"Feed My lambs."

Jesus asked him a second time:

"Simon, son of Jonah, do you love Me?" (John 21:16)

Peter answered the same way, with sincerity and without embellishment:

"Yes, Lord; You know that I love You."

Jesus said to him:

"Tend My sheep."

The third time, Jesus pressed the question, and the text says that Peter was grieved—not because Jesus was rejecting him, but because He was touching a wound still open:

"Simon, son of Jonah, do you love Me?" (John 21:17)

Peter, hurt but honest, replied:

"Lord, You know all things; You know that I love You."

Jesus said to him:

"Feed My sheep."

With each response, Jesus not only forgave his past; He restored his calling. That encounter did not expose Peter to shame him, but to restore him. Shame was replaced with responsibility, and failure with commission.

Later, at Pentecost, that same Peter preached with boldness, and "about three thousand souls" believed *(Acts 2:41).*

The man who denied Jesus before a servant girl now proclaimed Him before multitudes. He became a pillar of the church and wrote letters calling believers to humility, hope, and endurance in suffering.

His impulsive nature was not eliminated; it was transformed. His strength was not annulled; it was redirected. Peter's story shows us that God does not discard our falls—He uses them to form leaders with compassion and firmness. But before reaching that place, Peter had to walk on waters that revealed his cracks.

WHEN JESUS APPEARS ON THE WATER

The night was still far gone. The waves kept crashing. The boat creaked. The disciples were rowing—exhausted, soaked, trembling. Suddenly, in the darkness, a figure came toward them, walking on the water. Gripped by fear, they cried out, "It is a ghost!" This is how we often react when Jesus shows up in a way we do not expect: we interpret rescue as a threat.

But He spoke before desperation could take over:

"Be of good cheer! It is I; do not be afraid". (Matthew 14:27)

Courage for the heart, identity for the mind, and peace for the soul. Jesus reveals Himself before performing any miraculous act. His presence is the answer before circumstances change.

The disciples were caught between awe and fear. Imagine being utterly exhausted, rowing for hours, drenched, hands shaking, and suddenly hearing the Master—seemingly walking on the waves—telling you not to be afraid. Some covered their faces; others wept. Peter, true to his character, did not remain frozen in the initial shock. His mind began to process the impossibility his eyes were seeing. His heart wavered between the desire to go toward Jesus and the fear of sinking. It is in those tense seconds that the bravest decisions are made. We recognize Christ's voice, but we also feel the wind.

The decision to trust or to withdraw is made in a single heartbeat.

"LORD, IF IT IS YOU..." — THE REQUEST THAT CHANGED EVERYTHING

In the middle of the wind, Peter spoke up: *"Lord, if it is You, command me to come to You on the water."* He did not ask for a sign, nor for the storm to calm down, nor for Jesus to get into the boat. He asked for a word. While the others remained afraid, Peter dared to test whether that "I am" was enough to step onto the impossible.

This is the essence of mature faith: it does not ask for the storm to change; it asks Jesus to speak. Doubt looks for guarantees; faith looks for direction. There are moments when faith is not measured by the absence of fear, but by the boldness to ask for a word in the middle of fear.

"Come" — A Word That Sustains the Impossible

If we think about it, this scene feels like a practical class no one signed up for, yet everyone ends up taking. Welcome to the school of Jesus, where you get the exam first and the explanation later. That's how it works: first the storm, then the lesson. And you know what? We have all had that moment of "What if I sink?" But faith changes the script: "What if God holds me?" Fear is nothing more than faith placed in the wrong *"what if."* It's like paying rent on an apartment you're never going to live in.

What's striking is that Jesus did not give a ten-step manual on how to walk on water. He didn't say, "Look, Peter, first breathe, then lean your body at a 45-degree angle…" None of that. He released just one word: **"Come."** And that was enough. A single word loaded with all the power of heaven. We ask for details, and He responds with direction.

And pay attention: what seems greatest in human eyes is not always greatest in God's eyes. The centurion *(Matthew 8:5–13),* who asked on behalf of his servant, showed greater faith by staying in his house than many who boasted of great feats. Sometimes the strongest faith does not shout; it stands firm in silence, trusting that one word from Jesus is enough.

In the end, the central lesson is this: our security does not depend on the steadiness of our steps, but on the strength of the hands that hold us. Like a perfect receiver who never misses, Jesus is ready to catch us when we dare to take the leap. Our faith does not rest on our ability to walk on water, but on His power to keep us from sinking. God does not always tell us how to walk; He simply gives the call. Our methods look for steps and guarantees, but Jesus responds with direction.

LET GO OR YOU SINK

Peter obeyed the verb and stepped down from the boat. Before the miracle, there was an act of letting go. He had to release the wood he knew in order to step onto water he had never tried. The hardest step was not on the water; it was out of the boat.

We all have a boat: a security, a habit, a fear, an opinion, an excuse, an inner voice, a "just in case." Faith begins when you let go of what keeps you floating by logic in order to trust what keeps you walking by obedience. If you don't let go of the boat, you don't walk; if you don't walk, you stagnate; if you stagnate, you sink. Let go or you sink. That simple—and that deep.

WHEN THE WIND SHOUTS LOUDER THAN FAITH

Peter stepped out and began to walk on the water toward Jesus. In the biblical story, there had been crossings of waters: Moses and the people of Israel crossed the Red Sea on dry ground, when "the waters were divided" and *"the children of Israel went into the midst of the sea on dry ground"* (Exodus 14:21–22). Joshua and the entire nation crossed the Jordan when *"the waters which came down from upstream stood still"* and *"the people crossed over on dry ground"* (Joshua 3:16–17). Later, Elijah and Elisha struck the Jordan River and *"the waters were divided this way and that, and the two of them crossed over on dry ground"* (2 Kings 2:8, 14).

But no one—besides Jesus—had ever walked on the waves themselves. That privilege belongs only to the Lord of nature, who, "walking on the sea," came toward His disciples in the midst of the storm *(Matthew 14:25)*.

However, while Peter was walking, he began to look at the wind: *"But when he saw that the wind was boisterous, he was afraid...."* Peter did have faith, but not enough to keep his gaze fixed. The problem was not noticing the wind; it was stopping looking at Jesus. What you look at determines what you feel; your focus is your spiritual rudder. While Peter looked at Jesus, he walked; when he looked at the wind, he began to sink. He went from being a water-walking champion to "Peter the submarine," not because Jesus failed, but because Peter changed his reference point.

The same happens to us: today we don't need the waves of Galilee to distract us; we have news that looks like horror movies, social media full of comparisons, and friends who are experts in "what if everything goes wrong?" Faith is not closing your eyes to the storm; it is choosing the right reference. Less screen, more Word; fewer complaints, more gratitude. And if you're going to sink into something, let it be into His grace—not into your distractions.

"Lord, Save Me!" — My Own Cry

As he began to sink, Peter cried out, "Lord, save me!" It is one of the most effective prayers in the Bible: short, sincere, without protocol. He did not recite a speech; he simply cried out his need. This is where my own story connects.

From my youth, I have sought to know the will of God. I longed to hear His voice for every step. During that season, I was in a serious relationship with a Christian girlfriend: we shared our faith, a love for music, and singing. She was a wonderful person. However, in a time of prayer, I clearly sensed that this relationship was not part of God's plan for me.

It was not because of anything wrong with her, but because of a different calling that I needed to follow. Obedience meant letting go of something good in order to embrace something better, even when that "better" was still unknown.

When I decided to end the relationship, well-meaning friends said I was acting emotionally and that God had not spoken to me. Those opinions planted doubts: "Was it really God? What if I'm wrong? What if I let go of something God wanted for me?" That phrase—"why did you doubt?"—became a mirror. I discovered that doubt grows when I listen too much to the crowd and not enough to Christ. Jesus does not only rebuke doubt; He redirects it. When we cry out, "Lord, save me," He stretches out His hand. I learned that faith is not the absence of doubts, but the decision to bring them to God and keep walking. The same voice that said **"Come"** to Peter still says, **"Trust."** If I fall, He lifts me up. That is the heart of the gospel: it is not about my ability to stay afloat, but about His grace to sustain me.

Obedience is not always a moment in the past; even today, when I pray, I go to God asking for direction. There are decisions, both big and small, in which I still say, "Lord, if it is You, speak to me." The life of faith does not have an expiration date. It remains a process of letting go of the boat, moving forward in the midst of the wind, feeling fear, and yet trusting that His hand is extended. And throughout this journey, God has shown me His faithfulness to the fullest. It is not a sin to have questions; the problem is remaining stuck because of them.

In the middle of that process of letting go, He had prepared for me Milka, the woman who today is my friend, counselor, ally, companion, and wife. Our relationship was—and still is—

a reminder that God never asks you to release something without having something better—more aligned with His purpose—waiting for you ahead. Milka did not arrive as a reward for letting go; she arrived as evidence that obedience opens doors to the unimaginable. And to this day, when I face new winds, she stands by my side, reminding me to whom we belong and where we are going.

SINKING OR SYNCHRONIZING — TWO PERSPECTIVES

The scene of Peter sinking reminds us that what we see is not always what is truly happening. From his perspective, the sea was swallowing him. From Jesus' perspective, it was the perfect moment for Peter to align his faith with the rhythm of His grace. The same happens to us: we think we are drowning in debt, in problems, in anxiety, but perhaps what God is actually doing is synchronizing us with His pace.

He waits for us to lift our voice and cry out, "Save me!"—not to expose us, but to extend His hand.

Synchronization is alignment: my step with His step, my rhythm with His rhythm. Worship, prayer, and community are like a spiritual metronome that calibrates my heart to His. When I find that rhythm, the waves do not disappear, but they stop dictating the direction.

I may have water up to my ankles, but my eyes remain fixed on His face. And then, instead of sinking into anxiety, I sink into His presence—and there I discover that His peace is a better life preserver than any boat.

"It is not always about floating; sometimes what saves you is sinking... into His grace."

THE HAND THAT IS NEVER LATE

The moment Peter cried out, Jesus stretched out His hand and held him: "And immediately Jesus stretched out His hand and caught him..." "Immediately" is the rhythm of grace. He did not arrive when Peter mastered the technique or when he stopped trembling. He arrived at exactly the right moment. Jesus does not let fall those who dare to step out in faith.

Here the metaphor of the loading bar comes in: there are days when my heart feels like a screen with a loading bar stuck at 20 percent. I look at my life and everything seems frozen. Paused projects, unanswered prayers, unfulfilled promises. I want to click so it will just move already. But divine synchronization does not depend on my impatience. Not seeing progress does not mean the process has stopped. God is not frozen; He is working in the background. Isaiah said it: "My thoughts are higher than your thoughts, and My ways higher than your ways."

Synchronization depends on closeness: when I disconnect from His presence, it is like losing signal—nothing downloads. But when I draw near through prayer, worship, and obedience, heaven begins to download what has already been prepared. God's timing sometimes feels exasperating, but He knows when to release the update. My task is to stay connected: pray, serve, give thanks, trust. What is invisible is not nonexistent; it is a process in motion. Even if it seems frozen, heaven's loading bar never gets stuck halfway.

WHY DID YOU DOUBT?— THE FINAL MIRROR

When Jesus took hold of Peter, He said to him: "You of little faith, why did you doubt?" His question was not meant to shame him, but to reveal him. "Little faith" does not always refer to quantity; sometimes it refers to duration. Peter had faith—enough to step out of the boat. The problem was sustaining it.

The contrast appears in the centurion who pleaded for his servant: he did not need Jesus to enter his house or perform a dramatic gesture; he trusted that a word would be enough. That is great faith—the kind that remains steady when there is no applause.

True faith is not only the heroic leap out of the boat; it is also the patience of the one who keeps rowing, even when the arms grow heavy. In the end, our security does not rest on how firm our steps are, but on how strong the hand is that holds us. That hand does not tremble, even when ours lets go.

The story ends with Jesus and Peter stepping into the boat, and the wind ceasing. The storms were not sent to destroy them, but to teach them who He is—and who they are in Him. The other disciples may have remained in the boat, criticizing or admiring; they are not condemned, but they did not live the same experience.

We all face opposing winds; we all doubt. The question "Why did you doubt?" is not meant to embarrass us; it is meant to remind us that there is a reason to trust. The One who multiplied the loaves is the same One who walks on water. He does not abandon us; He invites us to know Him more deeply.

Every trial is an opportunity to synchronize our hearts with His faithfulness.

LETTING GO OF NEGATIVE THOUGHTS

The wind that shook the disciples is like those internal and external voices that sometimes drive us crazy. One day it is the inner whisper saying, "You're not enough." Another day it's a careless comment from someone else. And sometimes, we are our own harshest critics, beating ourselves harder than anyone else ever could.

The problem is that we cling to thoughts that weigh like stones. Imagine rowing with all your strength while a rock is tied around your neck. Not even Michael Phelps survives that. Letting go does not mean denying what happened or pretending it didn't hurt; letting go means deciding that the memory, the offense, or the criticism will not determine the direction of your boat.

And let's be clear—not everything needs to be spiritualized. Therapy can help us identify the traps of the mind, while the Word of God reminds us of the truth that endures. It's a powerful combination: psychology exposes the lie, theology affirms the truth. When I release "I am a victim" and embrace "I am a child of God," my soul becomes lighter, like a balloon rising into the air. And then what Paul wrote becomes real:

"Be renewed in the spirit of your mind".

(*Ephesians 4:23*)

Every day is a filter: which thoughts do I let in, and which do I throw out with the trash? If I don't learn to choose, my "what ifs" turn into chains. But if I release what weighs me down, I begin to float, to move forward, and to discover that the storm was not meant to sink me, but to teach me how to sail lighter.

THE RESPONSE OF THE HEART

At some point, we are all Peter. When we obey without fully understanding. When we let go of what once made us feel secure. When we feel the wind pushing against us. When we take a step and then begin to wobble. When we cry out, **"Save me!"** When Jesus holds us without hesitation.

The invitation remains the same: **"Come."** Come—even if the wind is still blowing. Come—even if fear is loud. Come—even if not everything is clear. Come—even if you are trembling Come—even if you make mistakes. Come—even if you have sunk before.

Let go, or you will sink.
But if you do sink… cry out.

PRAYER

Lord Jesus,
You know my uncertain steps and the moments when, like Peter, I dare to step out of the boat but lose myself in the wind. In the middle of my doubts, speak to my heart again. Remind me that Your calling does not depend on my strength, but on Your grace; that You did not call me because I am perfect, but because You love me.

Today I place in Your hands my fears, my "what ifs," and

everything that causes me to sink. Hold my faith when it is fragile, steady my feet when they tremble, and give me courage to walk toward where You are calling me.

Lord, if my gaze drifts, bring it back to You. If my heart doubts, whisper Your peace to me. And when I sink, do not allow me to remain beneath the waves—take me by the hand and lead me to the place where Your purpose awaits me.

May every step—on solid ground or upon the waters—draw me closer to Your voice
and lead me to live the calling for which I was created.

In Your name, Jesus. Amen.

CHAPTER 10

WHY ARE YOU WORRIED AND TROUBLED?

THE INNER NOISE

MARTHA

WHEN THE SOUL WON'T BE QUIET

"Now it happened as they went that He entered a certain village; and a certain woman named Martha welcomed Him into her house. And she had a sister called Mary, who also sat at Jesus' feet and heard His word. But Martha was distracted with much serving, and she approached Him and said, "Lord, do You not care that my sister has left me to serve alone? Therefore tell her to help me. And Jesus answered and said to her, Martha, Martha, you are worried and troubled about many things. But one thing is needed, and Mary has chosen that good part, which will not be taken away from her".

Luke 10:38-42

Sometimes it isn't the noise of the world that steals our peace, but the persistent echo of our own mind. It doesn't take an earthquake, a crisis, or a crowd—just a mental list that won't stop playing.

The dishes are missing.
The report is unfinished.
The money is short.
Time is running out.

And without realizing it, that list becomes an invisible chain dragging the soul down. Martha lived right there—in that space between devotion and obligation. She had Jesus in her house, but not in her attention. She had the Master under her roof, but her heart was stuck at the sink. And if we're honest, more than one of us has prayed with a spoon in hand and anxiety in our chest.

We serve God with busy hands and a divided heart. We love

190

His presence, but we run so hard that when we finally arrive, we're already exhausted.

WHEN SERVICE BECOMES NOISE

Martha wasn't doing anything wrong. She wasn't sinning or rebelling. She was serving. She was doing what any of us would do if the Son of God showed up unannounced for dinner with twelve guests (and none of them brought dessert). The problem wasn't the work—it was the distraction. The text says that "Martha was distracted with much serving." The word distracted in the original carries the idea of being "pulled in many directions."

That's exactly what happens when the soul is torn between what's urgent and what's eternal. And suddenly, in the middle of the hustle, Jesus seems to fade into the background. He's still there—but our mind isn't.

If Martha were alive today, she might wear an apron with her name embroidered on it and a smartwatch reminding her how many steps she's taken serving the Lord. And I don't doubt that Jesus would smile as He watched her rush from one place to another—but He would wait for just the right moment to say to her, gently:

—Martha, Martha... I'm not calling you to run faster, but to notice that you're running in circles.

THE LIST THAT NEVER ENDS

Martha represents all of us who love God but have confused **activity with intimacy**—those of us who think that the more we do, the more we please Him. And yet, Jesus does not measure love by tasks completed, but by attentive hearts.

That afternoon in Bethany, Martha had a list: the bread, the wine, the chairs, the tablecloth, the plates, the utensils, the hungry disciples, and probably a sibling who wasn't helping (because there's always one). And somewhere between so many priorities, the **Guest** became just another item.

Not the center—just number eleven on the agenda.

Jesus is not offended by our lists.
What grieves Him is when those lists **pull us away from Him.**

*Because serving without listening eventually leaves us empty, and working without worship makes us forget **who we started doing all this for.***

THE ECHO OF WHAT'S MISSING

Sometimes we don't need **more things to do;** we need **fewer things that distract us.** Because it's not physical exhaustion that steals our peace—it's soul fatigue. That invisible weariness that cannot be healed by sleeping, but only by stopping.

Martha thought everything had to be perfect, but Jesus did not ask for a formal dinner. He did not come to inspect the menu; He came to **feed hearts.** And while Mary was listening, Martha was listening to her own mind. One was speaking with the Master; the other was speaking with her anxiety.

Perhaps, if you had been in that house, you would have seen the same contrast we see today in our own lives: a corner of worship and a kitchen of worry. Both real. Both necessary.

But one far more eternal than the other.

THE DAY HEAVEN KNOCKED ON THE DOOR

That day began like any other in Bethany. The sun rested on the rooftops, chickens clucked in the background, and the air smelled of flour and firewood. But in the middle of the routine, a voice ran through the village: **"Jesus is coming!"** And when someone said *"Jesus is coming,"* it wasn't just any visitor. It was as if heaven itself were drawing near to the dust.

Martha, always diligent, reacted immediately. If Jesus was passing through her village, how could she not receive Him? And if He was entering her home, how could she not prepare everything? Without thinking twice, she opened the doors of her house—and also the doors of her responsibility.

The text says that "Martha welcomed Him into her home," but if we imagine the scene, we might add: "and she also welcomed Him with an apron on and a list in her hand." While Jesus and His disciples settled in the courtyard, Martha began organizing her small army of pots, ladles, and expectations. The men talked, Mary sat near Jesus, and the air filled with divine conversation.

Martha, on the other hand, filled herself with tasks. In one corner there was laughter; in another, the clanging of cookware. And in the middle of it all, the most human contrast of all: one listens, the other rushes. One pauses, the other accelerates. One seeks a word; the other seeks approval.

There is something both beautiful and dangerous about being "the one who gets things done." That need for everything to work, for no one to go hungry, for nothing to be missing. Martha didn't want to impress; she wanted to honor. But in the attempt, honor turned into a burden.

The table was almost ready, the bread in the oven, the wine poured—but something inside her began to boil more than the soup. She looked at Mary, seated at the feet of the Master, and felt emotions piling up: exhaustion, frustration, and perhaps a hint of envy disguised as fairness. Because when we are worn out, another person's silence can sound like irresponsibility.

It's not hard to imagine the scene: Martha enters with her hands on her hips, sweat on her brow, and with that tone of someone trying to be respectful—but who can't hold it in any longer:

"Lord, do You not care that my sister has left me to serve alone? Tell her to help me."

It is a prayer disguised as a complaint, a plea mixed with reproach. In other words: "Jesus, I'm tired of doing what's right and no one noticing." It sounds spiritual, but it carries the weight of something many of us feel—the sensation of serving much and being seen little.

Jesus looks at her with tenderness. He doesn't correct her harshly. He doesn't accuse her of lacking faith. He answers with love, and His response travels through centuries to reach us today:

"Martha, Martha, you are worried and troubled about many things; but one thing is needed."

These words are not a rebuke; they are a rescue. They do not come from someone irritated, but from someone who loves her too much to let her drown in her own effort. "Martha, Martha…"—as one repeats a name to slow a racing soul—"you don't need to do more; you need to be here."

How many times has the Lord wanted to tell us the same

thing in the middle of our hurried days. When we run with an agenda in hand, a scattered heart, and a divided mind, He doesn't ask for more speed—He invites us into stillness. He doesn't demand results; He invites us to rest.

Jesus does not despise Martha's work—after all, someone had to cook.

> But He is calling her to remember that the priority is not what we do **for Him,** but what we allow Him to do **in us.**

LISTS THAT SPEAK FOR THEMSELVES

Martha's problem was not service—it was the emotional overload of feeling that everything depended on her. In her mind there was no room for calm, because every thought came with a reminder attached. And if you've ever gone to bed with your mind running faster than your feet, you know what that feels like: the body shuts down, but the list stays awake.

"This is missing."
"I should have done that."
"What if I don't make it?"

Sometimes no one even needs to demand more from you—you remind yourself every five minutes. Martha didn't have a phone, but her mind was in notification mode. Every thought buzzed with a new task. Today, we would call her a multitasker—the kind of woman who can fry food, talk on the phone, correct the children, and pray for the neighbor all at the same time. And yet, though she looked more efficient, deep down she was more empty.

Because when everything becomes urgent, nothing feels important.

Jesus didn't ask her to turn off the stove; He asked her to turn on her heart. Because it is not the same thing to cook for Christ as it is to cook with Christ present. The first one exhausts you; the second one renews you. The first leaves you with a sense of duty fulfilled; the second with the certainty that you have been with Him.

If we think about it, we all have an inner kitchen full of noise. Sometimes it's not a pot that's clanging, but guilt; not a spoon hitting the pan, but haste. We do good things, but from a worn-out heart. And when that happens, the soul begins to complain: "Doesn't anyone see what I do? Doesn't anyone help? Doesn't anyone say thank you?" We become martyrs of our own expectations.

I've heard many people say, "I serve God, but I feel like no one notices." And perhaps Jesus would answer them the same way He answered Martha: "Yes, I see it—but more than applauding what you do, I want to heal why you do it." Because serving out of love heals, but serving for approval makes us sick.

If Martha had had a virtual assistant, she probably would have said, "Alexa, add to my list: mop the floor, bake bread, feed twelve disciples, and remind my sister that she exists." But not even Alexa could handle that. When the list never stops, it doesn't matter how many tasks you complete—there will always be one more waiting for you, and always the same feeling: it's not enough.

Jesus doesn't tell Martha to stop serving; He teaches her to prioritize from the soul.

Only one thing is necessary.
Not two. Not ten. Not the whole list.
One.

But that one thing changes everything. Because when you put Jesus first, everything else falls into its proper place. The world has convinced us that we are worth what we produce, but the Kingdom reminds us that we are worth who we are in Him. Martha thought she was honoring Christ with what she did; she never imagined that He would feel more honored if she simply sat down. Not because He despises work, but because He loves the worker more.

Jesus is not looking for employees of the Kingdom, but for sons and daughters who enjoy His presence.

Martha's anxiety had a last name: comparison. She looked at Mary and felt that her effort wasn't enough. And though we may not say it out loud, many of us live that same silent battle—comparing what we do with what others seem to enjoy.

Martha served. Mary listened. And Jesus loved them both. But Martha couldn't enjoy that love because she filtered everything through her performance. There's a phrase we could write on the wall of Martha's kitchen:

"Don't compete in an area where God never asked you to compare."

The problem is not serving differently; the problem is losing peace trying to serve the same way. Mary wasn't better—she was just in a different moment. And Jesus wasn't grading either of them; He was simply reminding them of what matters most: being present. What Martha saw as irresponsibility, Jesus saw as worship. What she called "wasting time," He called "gaining rest." Because sometimes the greatest faith is not shown by running, but by staying still.

Martha represents the heart that loves so much it forgets to enjoy. And that accelerated love—without pause—ends up exhausting even the holiest things. But Jesus came to teach her—and us—that grace does not run; it rests. Grace does not say, "Do more," it says, "Stay here."

WHEN GOD TURNED DOWN THE NOISE

I've had my own Martha days too—just with a phone in my hand.

When I finished the book Nicolás, my original prayer had been clear:

"Lord, let this book touch generations. Let the grandchildren, the great-grandchildren, and even those not yet born come to know the God Nicolás served, and may his legacy continue."

That was the intention.

But as soon as the book was released, something in me quietly shifted focus. Without realizing it, my list was no longer: "May Your name be known, Lord,"
but instead:

"How many likes does it have today?"
"How many books sold this week?"
"Did someone leave a new review?"

I wasn't preparing a dinner, but I was just as anxious and troubled. I wasn't running from the stove to the table, but from one notification to another. I opened Facebook, closed Facebook, opened it again. I checked sales, refreshed the page, checked again.

And the hardest part is this: God had already spoken to me about writing long before that. I already had titles for future books. I had already begun writing Is There Anyone? The direction was clear—but my mind got stuck in the hallway of likes.

I said I wanted to touch generations, but I lived focused on right now.

I prayed for grandchildren and great-grandchildren who might one day read Nicolás's story, yet my peace depended on how many people clicked "like" in the first twenty-four hours.

Until the Lord— with the same tenderness He used with Martha—began to speak to me. Not with an audible voice, but with a holy discomfort:

"Saul, you're looking at the wrong number."

So I made a simple decision—radical for me:
one week without Facebook or any social media.
No checking sales.
No "just a quick look."
No "let me see how it's doing."

That week was like turning off the noise in the kitchen. Suddenly, everything got quieter.

In those days, something lit up where there had only been notifications before. My imagination and God's direction crossed paths again. I read four books (audiobooks, to be precise). My mind refocused on what truly mattered: writing.

But I didn't just keep writing the book.

Something God had spoken to me in my youth—something I had almost filed away—began to wake up: songs.

Years ago, God had told me He would give me songs. And honestly, for a long time I thought that chapter had closed. But it wasn't that God had delayed—it was that I had interrupted the flow of the Spirit, distracted by likes, sales, and comparisons.

That week without social media, lyrics and melodies began to be born. While the digital world went silent, the creative voice of the Spirit grew louder. It wasn't magic—it was space. It wasn't that God finally remembered me; it was that I finally stopped distracting myself.

I realized something very similar to what Martha lived:

I wasn't doing something wrong—the problem was from where I was doing it.

Writing a book isn't wrong.
Promoting a project isn't wrong.
Using social media isn't wrong.

But when the heart begins to depend on those things to feel valuable, it stops being service and becomes noise.

That week I understood that Jesus wasn't asking me to stop writing or stop dreaming—He was asking me to sit down again and listen. To remember that my calling didn't begin with a like, but with His word. That my value isn't measured in sales, but in obedience.

And maybe, just like me, you've had your own digital Martha moment—not in a kitchen, but on a screen. Not with pots and ladles, but with apps and notifications.

If that's you, let me tell you something from my own experience:

sometimes the miracle isn't that the post goes viral,

but that the soul becomes quiet.

> *That God turns down the noise outside, so He can heal what inside has been running without rest.*

WHEN THE SOUL LEARNS TO LET GO

With time, Martha understood something that isn't learned by cooking, but by surrendering: there are battles that are not won by doing more, but by stopping the fight. Sometimes the soul has to unlearn its rhythm before it can truly rest in God.

Martha—the woman who once complained in the kitchen—does not disappear from the story. She appears again in another scene, and this time she is no longer wrestling with pots and pans, but with death itself.

Her brother Lazarus had fallen ill. As always, she acted quickly. She sent word to Jesus:

"Lord, behold, he whom You love is sick". (John 11:3)

But the Master did not arrive when expected. Days passed, the illness worsened, and the miracle did not come. Lazarus died—and with him, hope seemed to die as well.

When Jesus finally arrived in Bethany—four days late, according to the human calendar—Martha went out to meet Him. She didn't wait for Him to call her. She went out wounded, exhausted, but with enough faith left to speak. And there, on that dusty road, she meets Jesus again. Not as the anxious and troubled woman from the kitchen, but as someone who has learned—through pain—that control has limits.

"Lord, if You had been here, my brother would not have died."

In that sentence, her whole heart is exposed: faith, frustration, grief. But what she says next reveals the transformation:

"But even now I know that whatever You ask of God, God will give You".

(John 11:22)

There it is.

Martha is no longer asking Jesus to correct her sister with a spoon in her hand; she is declaring trust in front of a tomb. The same woman who once asked Jesus to intervene in a domestic dispute now entrusts Him with resurrection. The process changed her. What once troubled her now sustained her. Hurry gave way to patience, control to rest, the list to silence.

It is beautiful to realize that Jesus did not correct Martha to humiliate her, but to prepare her. In the first scene, He was training her for this one.

Because the one who learns to rest in His presence will know how to wait in His absence.

Jesus knew that one day she would seek Him in the midst of grief—and that this time she would not ask Him to scold anyone, but to do the impossible. Martha, the practical woman who measured life in tasks, learned that God's timing is not measured in lists, but in promises. And that even when the clock says late, heaven is never behind schedule.

She understood it when Jesus said:
"I am the resurrection and the life."

Not "I bring the solution," but "I am."
Not a method, but a person.
Not a schedule, but a presence.

How beautiful it is when the soul stops saying, "If You had been here," and begins to say, "I know You are here." That is the leap Martha made—the invisible step from productivity to presence. And though she may still have glanced at the clock from time to time, she now understood that the miracle does not depend on her punctuality, but on His power.

Perhaps that is why Jesus loved being in Bethany so much. Because there, He didn't just eat—He taught people how to rest.

In Martha's house we learn that faith does not always cook instant miracles; sometimes it lets them ferment until the heart softens. In the first scene, Martha holds control; in the second, she releases it. In the first, she seeks help to organize; in the second, she seeks Jesus to resurrect.

The difference is that now she no longer gives God instructions—she gives Him space. She no longer says, "Tell her to help me," but simply, "I know You can."

That is spiritual maturity: moving from directing heaven to resting in it.

Many of us pray like Martha the first time:
"Lord, do this. Fix that. Hurry this up."

And Jesus answers us as He did then:
"I didn't call you to manage—I called you to trust."

It's not that you can't organize; it's that you can't control what is eternal. And the sooner you understand that, the sooner you will rest.

If the first Martha looks like our daily lives, the second represents what the Spirit wants to form in us: a heart that knows when to serve and when to sit, when to run and when to weep, when to speak and when to wait.

And the most freeing truth of all: Jesus does not love Mary more than Martha, nor the one who sings more than the one who cooks. He simply wants both to learn how to be with Him.

The Rest That Cooks Miracles

Martha's story ends well, even though Scripture does not close it with a final period. Because when a heart learns to rest, its story never truly ends—it simply begins to beat more slowly, but more deeply.

Martha remained Martha: the organizer, the one who hosts, the one who wants everything to go well. Jesus did not come to erase her personality, but to heal it. He taught her that she could keep serving—but from calm, not from burden. That she could keep cooking—but with a rested soul. That she could remain active—without losing sight of the Guest.

The difference was not in what she did, but in where she did it from. Before, she served from pressure; now, from presence. Before, she tried to control the atmosphere; now, she allowed Christ to govern it. And when you learn that, even the kitchen becomes an altar. Because when the heart grows quiet, any space can become holy ground: an office, a classroom, a bedroom, a kitchen. Noise no longer matters if there is rest within.

Jesus did not come to teach Martha to stop serving, but to serve without losing herself. To enjoy the moment. To understand that the Kingdom does not require perfection, but attention. Because it is not the same to have Jesus in the house as it is to be in His presence. Sometimes He is right there—and the soul is too busy to notice.

Perhaps that is our greatest challenge today. It is not about having more time, but more awareness. Not about running less, but about running with purpose. Not about stopping work, but about working from a heart that has already rested in Him.

Jesus continues to repeat our name as He once did Martha's— with tenderness, not reproach:

"Saul, Saul... you are anxious and troubled about many things."

Not to shame you, but to invite you.

He does not shout—He whispers.
He does not accuse—He lifts.
He does not demand—He reminds:

"Only one thing is necessary."

And in that reminder is a freedom no productivity can offer. Because God's love is not earned by completing lists, but by clearing space to hear His voice. Grace does not measure you by what you achieve, but by how much you allow yourself to be loved.

If Martha could speak to us today, perhaps she would smile and say, "The oven can wait." And with her familiar humor, she might add, "Jesus doesn't need warm bread—He needs willing hearts."

Because in the end, when the soul rests in Christ, even unleavened bread tastes like heaven. Perhaps the greatest miracle in Bethany was not Lazarus walking out of the tomb, but Martha walking out of anxiety. Not the resurrection of a body, but the resurrection of a soul.

For there is no tomb deeper than an overloaded mind, and no freedom greater than a heart at peace.

That is how this story ends—not with applause, but with rest. Not with a completed list, but with a steady gaze.

Martha remains the same, but she no longer lives in a rush. Because she learned that faith also knows how to rest. And that sometimes, the truest worship is not doing something for Jesus, but allowing Jesus to do something in you.

So if today your life feels like a noisy kitchen, lower the flame, turn off the oven for a moment, and sit down.

The table can wait.
The soul cannot.

PRAYER

Lord Jesus,

You who entered Martha's house and knew the noise of her heart, enter my house and my mind today as well. You know how many times I have run from screen to screen, from list to list, searching for approval, numbers, and results—while my soul remained hungry for You. Forgive me for the times Your presence was so near, yet my attention so far away.

Today I choose to sit at Your feet. I want to let go of anxiety, comparison, and the need to be seen, and embrace the one thing that is necessary: listening to You.

Quiet the noise of my "likes," my tasks, and my fears, and reignite the fire of Your voice within me. May what I write, how I serve, what I publish, and what I dream be born not from my anxiety, but from Your direction.

Holy Spirit, teach me to live like a transformed Martha— working from rest, serving from peace, organizing without losing sight of the Guest.
May my home, my phone, my schedule, and my gifts become an altar where You are the center.

Today I place my lists in Your hands... and receive Your peace.

In the name of Jesus. Amen.

CHAPTER 11

WHAT DO YOU WANT ME TO DO FOR YOU?

GOD'S CALLING FOR THOSE LIVING ON THE ROADSIDE

BARTIMAEUS

WHEN JESUS STOPS
WHERE OTHERS WALK ON BY

I have always been struck by how this passage begins:

"Then they came to Jericho."

Just like that. No extra details. So simple. And yet, so loaded with history, meaning, and spiritual memory.

We have already walked through Jericho in this book. We have already heard the footsteps of an army circling walls, we have already seen stones fall through obedience, we have already understood that God uses old places to write new stories. I will not repeat what we have already discussed; but I do want you to understand this:

God passes through Jericho again because there are still walls that need to fall. Not walls of stone. Walls of identity. That verse is the doorway to the encounter that Mark narrates a few lines later *(Mark 10:46–52):* Bartimaeus, the son of Timaeus, sitting by the roadside.

This time there are no trumpets, no battle cries, no circles around the city. There is no ark, no organized lines, no instructions about how many days to march. The setting is similar, but the battle is different. Before, an entire people stood before a fortified city. Now, an ordinary crowd is walking along, and off to the side, one man who seems not to matter at all. There is only a crowd, a dusty road, and a blind man sitting on the edge.

This is the beautiful part: Jesus does not stop for the crowd. He stops for the one everyone else walks past. This is how God works. This is how He has always worked. And this is how He will continue to work: stopping in the places where you and I tend to speed up. Where we see "traffic," He sees hearts. Where we see "people," He sees names. Where we hear "noise," He hears a cry.

"Then they came to Jericho."

It is almost as if the Spirit were saying: "You already know this name, but look again. Do not assume that God is finished working in places where you think everything has already been said."

Because there are external Jerichos and internal Jerichos. There are walls made of stone, and walls made of sentences: "This is just how you are," "This is where you got stuck," "You will never get past this." And Jesus enters Jericho not merely to cross a city, but to cross the invisible barrier that has kept a man sitting on the roadside for years.

BLINDNESS IS NOT EXPLAINED: IT IS LIVED

The Bible describes Bartimaeus with four words: *"Bartimaeus, the blind man, the son of Timaeus."* How easy it is to write "the blind man." But how difficult it is to live it. Behind that title are years of adaptation, grief, and learning the hard way. When we preach this story, we often rush through it: Jesus passes by, the man cries out, Jesus heals him—end of story. But the miracle lasts seconds. The reality of living with a disability lasts years.

The Bible gives us no details about his childhood, but anyone who understands even a little about the human condition knows that behind the words "the blind man" there are parents learning to release expectations, a family reorganizing life around a new reality, and questions no one dares to say out loud:

"Why him?" "Will he ever be able to work?" "What will he be able to do when he grows up?"

There is a mother trying to explain to her child why he cannot play like the others, why he falls more often, why he needs to be guided by the hand. There is a father waking up in the middle of the night wondering what will become of him the day he is no longer there. There is a child learning to walk by textures, not by colors. There is frustration stored in small things others do without thinking: running, going out alone, reading, working, taking transportation without depending on anyone. In our home, we know this world. Not by theory. Not by documentaries. By life.

Our oldest son, Christian, is deaf and has limited vision. He lives on his own, works, grows, and gets up every day with courage, but his life is filled with adjustments invisible to many: specialized transportation that must be coordinated in advance, instructions in large print just to be readable, communication through photos and whiteboards to avoid misunderstandings, memorized routes, corners navigated with patience, processes that for others are automatic but for him are projects that require planning.

I have seen the exhaustion that is never mentioned, the loneliness no one knows how to translate, the strength required simply to exist in a world that was not designed for you. I have seen what it means to carry a backpack no one can see on your back, but that weighs heavily on the soul.

Milka, as a special education teacher, has walked alongside children and families in those same struggles. She has sat in meetings where diagnoses are spoken with difficult words, she has embraced mothers who leave classrooms with tears mixed with love and fear, she has seen fathers weighed down by guilt over things they did not cause, she has listened to families ask whether their son or daughter will "ever be independent."

And I know that if she were writing this chapter, she would tell you something like this: "Living with a disability is not a spiritual weakness. Living with a disability is not a punishment. Living with a disability does not erase calling." Not everyone knows that pain. God does.

That is why this chapter needs to be written this way: human, honest, unfiltered, without religious clichés. Because blindness is not explained; it is lived. And the God of the Bible does not stay distant from that reality; He draws near, He stops, He asks, He listens, He touches, He calls.

SEATED BY THE ROAD: THE EDGE WHERE THE INVISIBLE SIT

The Bible adds a small detail, but one that opened my eyes: "...*was sitting by the road.*"

It does not say, "on the road." It does not say, "among the crowd." It does not say, "walking with them." It says, "by the road." On the edge. Where the ignored sit. That is the space where many live today: close to everything, but belonging to very little. Participating, but not integrated. Living, but on the margin.

People with disabilities know this place well. It is not only the physical limitation; it is the emotional experience of living on the edge of the system, the temple, the conversations, the opportunities. Close enough to hear what is happening, but not far enough inside to be part of the design.

"Seated by the road" is not a posture; it is a wound.

It is feeling outside the main flow. It is watching others move forward, speak, organize, serve, decide, while you wait for someone to remember to ask you something as simple as: "Do you want to come? Can you be here? What do you need?" And Jesus arrives there.

To that place. To that invisible chair. To that edge where the world leaves those it does not understand. It moves me to know that Jesus sees what the crowd does not see. He stops for the one sitting on the edge. People can get used to seeing someone on the same corner, day after day, until they become part of the scenery. But Jesus never turns anyone into scenery; to Him every person is a living story, the image of God, someone worth stopping the agenda for. Those things say more about His heart than a hundred miracles.

WHEN YOU CANNOT SEE, BUT YOU HEAR GOD DRAWING NEAR

The verse continues:
"And hearing that it was Jesus of Nazareth…"

Bartimaeus did not see Jesus. He did not see the crowd. He did not see faces, or the road, or the hands pushing him. But he heard. When you cannot see, other senses develop. When you cannot see what is coming, your soul becomes sensitive to what is sounding. When the eyes have few options, the ears learn to filter, to distinguish, to discern.

There are people who cannot see the future clearly, but they hear something in their spirit. A rumor. A hope. A step. Sometimes you cannot put it into words, but you sense that something is moving. Something inside you says, "Do not give up yet. This is not everything. It is not over."

Bartimaeus' faith began with a sound. Not with a sermon. Not with a vision. With a sound. And his heart said, "That is Him."

He did not see Jesus' face, but he recognized His name. He could not distinguish His sandals among so many, but he recognized the news: "It is Jesus of Nazareth who is passing by." And that was enough to ignite something that had been waiting for years; an opportunity to get up.

I wonder how many times Jesus has passed near us, but because our eyes are occupied, we do not hear Him. We are looking at screens, accounts, worries, statistics, diagnoses, and our hearts fill with images, but empty of listening. Faith does not always begin by seeing. Sometimes it begins by hearing.

"So then faith comes by hearing, and hearing by the word of God".
(Romans 10:17)

Bartimaeus did not have a printed Bible, or apps, or study notes, but he had something: a conviction that the name of Jesus was not just any name.

WHEN ALL YOU HAVE LEFT IS YOUR VOICE… AND THAT IS ENOUGH**

"…he began to cry out…"

That word began breaks me. Because no one starts shouting out of nowhere; you begin to cry out when you can no longer remain silent. There are silences that last weeks. There are silences that last years. But there comes a moment when the soul overflows. I do not know what his voice sounded like. Maybe hoarse, maybe trembling, maybe desperate. But I know it was not an elegant cry. It was a cry of need.

Cries like that are not born in the mouth.
They are born in the wound.

"Jesus, Son of David, have mercy on me!"

Look at his prayer. It is not sophisticated. It is not long. It has no decorations. It does not begin with an introduction. It does not explain his story. It does not present credentials or justify the request. He does not ask for money. He does not ask for pity. He does not ask for explanations. He asks for mercy.

When you have suffered for years, you know exactly what you need: mercy.

- Mercy is: **"Do not give me what I deserve;** give me what only Your heart can give."

- Mercy is: **"This is not about who I am;** it is about who You are."

- Mercy is: **"Even if everything has gone wrong for me,** I still believe that You are good."

And that is what Jesus knows how to give. There are prayers that sound perfect, but move nothing. And there are cries that sound messy, but move heaven.

What moves God is not grammar; it is the truth of the heart.

THE CROWD THAT TELLS HIM TO BE SILENT...
AND THE JESUS WHO CALLS HIM FORWARD

"And many rebuked him, telling him to be silent..."

The crowd does not hate Bartimaeus. They do not wish him harm. They simply want order. They want a quiet service. They want a neat procession. They want a walk without interruptions. They do not understand that Bartimaeus' cries are not disorder; they are desperate faith.

Sometimes religion does that: it confuses pain with interruption. It confuses need with annoyance. It confuses a cry with irreverence. Those who have never had to shout in order to be heard do not understand what it is like to live asking permission just to exist.

But the text says: *"...but he cried out all the more."*

When life has taken so much from you, you cannot afford to let it take your voice too. Maybe you are already out of strength, out of money, out of resources, out of explanations, out of answers. But you still have your voice. And as long as you have a voice, you still have something with which to respond to God.

And then what defines this chapter happens: "And Jesus stopped and commanded him to be called."

There are many things I do not know about heaven. But I know this: a sincere cry does not get lost in the air. It always reaches the heart of God.

And when God stops, everything changes. Where the crowd hears noise, Jesus hears faith. Where others see an inconvenience, He sees hunger for an encounter. Where some demand silence, He commands, "Call him."

This is the contrast of the whole story:
the people say, "Be quiet."
Jesus says, "Come."

THROWING OFF HIS CLOAK: THE ACT THAT DEFINES A CALLING

Every word matters. "Throwing off": he did not fold it calmly, he did not save it for later, he did not set it aside carefully. He threw it away. He released it with urgency, with haste, with decision.

"The cloak": it was not an accessory. It was his life. It was his bed, his covering, his income, his identity as a "blind beggar." With that cloak he gathered the coins people dropped. With that cloak he protected himself from the cold of the night. With that cloak he made space on the ground to sit.

That fabric said: "Here is someone who depends on alms to keep living." Throwing it away was saying: "I will not find my future where I found my past." Throwing it away was faith.

Not pretty faith. Practical faith. Risky faith The faith of someone who knows that if Jesus is calling him, He will not leave him the same.

There are cloaks we must also throw off today—not made of fabric, but heavy with meaning.

The cloak of "I can't."
The cloak of "I'm a burden."
The cloak of "no one sees me."
The cloak of "I will always live on the edge."
The cloak of "God has plans for others, not for me."

Jesus calls.
The cloak falls.
The journey begins.

When you decide to let go of what gave you a kind of "sad security"—that identity of victim, of invisible, of "this is who I am and this is where I stay"—you place yourself in position to discover that God has a new way of naming you.

THE QUESTION THAT RESTORES DIGNITY

"What do you want Me to do for you?"

I cannot read that question without feeling a knot in my throat. Jesus did not say, "I know what you need." "I will decide for you." "I will determine how to help you." Jesus said, "You tell Me."

Do you know how revolutionary that is? A world that is always deciding for people with disabilities is now standing before a Messiah who asks, "What do you want?"

Jesus does not only heal. Jesus dignifies. He does not speak over the disability. He speaks to the heart.

That is why this question is not rhetorical; it is restorative. With that question, Jesus gives Bartimaeus back something life had slowly taken from him: the ability to desire, to choose, to name his own longing.

Disability does not only affect the body; it also strikes the place of desire. Sometimes it kills dreams. Sometimes it convinces the heart that it is "better not to want too much, so you won't suffer too much."

Jesus comes and breaks that lie with a single sentence:

"What do you want Me to do for you?"

LORD, THAT I MAY RECEIVE MY SIGHT

"Rabboni, that I may receive my sight."

Bartimaeus did not ask for coins. He asked for the impossible. He asked to see again. It was a big desire. A deep desire. A desire he had carried for years. God loves stored-up desires. The ones that hurt. The ones that feel too big. The ones we only confess when He asks.

"That I may receive my sight." He does not say, "Give me something new that I never had." He says, "Give back to me what was once mine."

There are people who were born seeing and one day stopped seeing. There are those who once walked freely and one day could not anymore. There are those who heard clearly and one day sound began to fade. Asking to have restored what you lost hurts. Because when you say it out loud, you acknowledge how much you miss it.

But Jesus does not rebuke that request. He does not say, "Surviving should be enough." He does not say, "Don't be excessive." He does not say, "A handout will do." Jesus listens to that immense desire, and instead of reducing it, He honors it.

WHEN GOD OPENS YOUR EYES, HE OPENS THE WAY

"Then Jesus said to him, 'Go your way; your faith has made you well.' And immediately he received his sight and followed Jesus on the road".

(Mark 10:52)

The sentence is short, but layered with meaning.
"Go your way; your faith has made you well."
Faith was not seen when he was sitting down, nor when he was silent, but when he dared to cry out, to resist, to rise, to throw off his cloak, to ask for something great.

"And immediately he received his sight."
His eyes opened. Darkness broke. The world—once only sound and shadow—filled with shapes, faces, and color.
But the verse does not end there. Because the miracle does not end with sight.

"...and followed Jesus on the road."

He did not leave to celebrate.
He did not leave to tell everyone.

He did not go to the market.
He did not run to test everything he could now do.

He went after Jesus.

His sight was not only restored; his direction was redefined. The miracle lifted him from the roadside and placed him into the story. That is what God does: He places on the path those whom the world leaves on the edge.

When God opens your eyes, it is not only so you can see better. It is so you can walk differently.

A Calling for Those Who Live with Limitations

If you live with a disability, or if you love someone who does, hear this:
God does not see you as "the blind one," "the limited one," or "the one who needs help."
God sees you as someone called.
Someone needed.
Someone valuable.
Someone with purpose.

Your condition does not cancel your calling. Your pain does not erase your purpose. Your limitation does not invalidate your worth.

There are paths only you can walk because you see life in a way others do not. There are people only you will be able to embrace in a certain way, because you have felt in your own body what it means to be misunderstood. There are conversations only you will be able to have, because your scars speak a language others do not understand.

You are not an accident.
You are a design.

There is a verse that makes many uncomfortable, but for those of us who live close to disability, it confronts us and comforts us at the same time. When Moses gave God excuses because of his difficulty speaking, the Lord answered him:

> *"Who has made man's mouth? Or who makes the mute, the deaf, the seeing, or the blind? Have not I, the LORD?"*
>
> *(Exodus 4:11)*

God is not saying, "I hurt you for no reason." He is saying, "Even what the world calls a limitation, I see it, I know it, and I wrap it in My sovereignty."

Later, when the disciples asked Jesus who sinned so that a man was born blind—him or his parents—Jesus answered:

> *"Neither this man nor his parents sinned, but that the works of God should be revealed in him".*
>
> *(John 9:3)*

IT IS NOT PUNISHMENT. IT IS NOT A CURSE. IT IS NOT GOD'S "PLAN B."

Not only does the Bible say this; it is also echoed in the voices of many today. In a post, Hayden Daum, a deaf influencer, wrote:

"God did not make me deaf to silence me or mute me, but so that others might know Him and that His glory might be seen in me and through me."

He shared that he once thought his deafness was a barrier to sharing the gospel, but over time he understood that it is a bridge—the way God connects him with people.

"I have been called to reach others," he said, "and many times the strongest testimony is born from the quietest voice. I learned to listen to God not through sound, but through the surrender of the heart."

What a powerful declaration.

Disability is not a wall that prevents God from working; it is a stage where His glory can shine in ways others do not understand. Your body may have clear limits, but your spirit is not chained to that diagnosis.

God does not see you as a "case" the church has to manage.

He sees you as part of the body, as a necessary member, as someone through whom He wants to display His glory.

TO PARENTS, MOTHERS, AND FAMILY MEMBERS WHO CARRY MORE THAN THEY EVER SAY

This chapter is also for you. I know what it is like to love someone who needs more help. I know what it is like to fill out forms, attend medical appointments, therapies, adaptations, schools, evaluations, and make complicated decisions. I know what it is like to go to bed worried and wake up holding on to faith.

There are nights when the body is in bed, but the mind stays awake:
"Will they be okay?"
"Did I do everything I could?"
"What will happen when I'm no longer here?"

God sees you. God sustains you. God keeps you. God walks with you.

Jesus' question—"What do you want Me to do for you?"—is also for you:
—Lord, give me strength.
—Give me patience.
—Give me wisdom.
—Give me rest.
—Give my child a future.
—Surround them with people who will love them.

He does not judge you for feeling tired. He does not condemn you for crying in the bathroom. He does not scold you because sometimes you feel afraid. He looks at you with tenderness—and He stops for you too.

In the middle of your worries, He tells you:
"You are not raising this life alone. I am here. I am the God of covenant, the God of generations, the God who sees the end from the beginning."

To Those God Has Called to Serve People with Limitations

This chapter is a call for you: teachers, therapists, volunteers, leaders, pastors, coworkers, friends, employers. Maybe you do not live with a disability yourself, but God has placed you alongside someone who does.

Do not underestimate the value of your work. Do not underestimate the power of your patience. Do not underestimate the impact of your attention to detail.

Jesus did not teach inclusion. He embodied it. He stopped. He listened. He called. He asked. He touched.

And every time you make space, every time you adapt, every time you explain, every time you walk with someone, every time you choose to slow down so you can move at another's pace, you look like Him. Your ministry may not always have a microphone, but heaven is watching.

Every time you choose to see someone others pass by, it is as if Jesus stops again in Jericho through you. In many parts of the world, millions of deaf people have never had clear access to the gospel in their own sign language. It is not that they have rejected Jesus; it is that no one has explained Him in a way they can understand. That is not a technical detail. It is a Kingdom urgency.

When a church says, "We can't afford an interpreter," "We didn't think about that," "We don't have space for them," it may not be said with bad intentions, but the message many receive is: "You are not that important. You are not worth the effort." And that hurts more than we imagine.

God, on the other hand, looks at a deaf or blind person and thinks: "If you equip them, if you include them, if you serve alongside them… they will reach others you will never be able to touch."

There is something else I need to tell you if you serve—or feel drawn to serve—people with limitations: that stirring did not come from you; it is the Holy Spirit whispering for you to take a step. Sometimes you do not know where to begin, or you feel it is bigger than you, or you wonder if you will have enough patience, creativity, or resources. Listen carefully: obedience is enough. When you take the first step, God opens the rest. He will give you the creativity to invent what does not yet exist, the wisdom to adapt what already does, and the grace to implement what once seemed impossible. It does not matter if the road feels uphill; in this calling, willingness weighs more than ability. If your heart is available, God will take care of the rest.

And remember: it is not about doing everything for them, but about walking with them, serving alongside them, and recognizing that they, too, have been called to make disciples.

THE BLINDNESS WE ALL CARRY

All throughout the Bible there are clear signs that God sees, loves, and calls those who live with limitations:

"Then the eyes of the blind shall be opened, and the ears of the deaf shall be unstopped" (Isaiah 35:5);

Jesus healing a man who was deaf and mute (Mark 7:31–37);

inviting "the poor, the crippled, the lame, and the blind" to His banquet (Luke 14:13).

The message is unmistakable: **they have always been close to the heart of God.** Not all of us are physically blind. But all of us have areas where we do not see: we do not see our sin, our worth, our need, the pain of others, or what God wants to do.

The story of Bartimaeus reminds us that the most dangerous blindness is not in the eyes, but in the soul. You can have perfect eyesight and a hardened heart. You can read the Bible and never allow it to read you. You can see people, yet fail to see their pain.

When Jesus opens Bartimaeus' eyes, He is inviting us to ask for the same thing—even if we can see physically:

"Lord, open my eyes."
"Open my eyes to see my need for You."
"Open my eyes to see the value of others."
"Open my eyes to see those who are sitting by the road."

And to everyone—everyone—Jesus asks the same question:

"What do you want Me to do for you?"

ANSWER... HE HAS ALREADY STOPPED

Bartimaeus cried out. The crowd tried to silence him. Jesus stopped. And his life changed forever.

That same Jesus is passing by your Jericho today.

It does not matter if you are on the edge.
It does not matter if you feel invisible.

It does not matter if others do not understand your struggle. It does not matter if you have been sitting by the road for years. He stops. He calls you. He asks you. And now it is your turn to respond.

What do you want Him to do for you?

Whatever it is... ask Him.

He is already standing in front of you.

PRAYER

Lord Jesus,
You who stopped in Jericho and listened to the cry of a man sitting by the roadside, stop today on our path as well. Open our ears to hear You, open our eyes to see You, and open our hearts to respond to You.

We bring before You every person living with a limitation, every family walking with love and weariness, and every servant You have called to walk alongside them. Give them renewed strength, surprising wisdom, transforming creativity, and sustaining peace.

Restore weary hearts, return lost hope, and redeem every area where we have lived on the edge. Ask us once again, Lord: "What do you want Me to do for you?" And give us the courage to answer You in faith.

May Your light open our eyes, may Your love open our paths, and may Your grace teach us to see as You see.
In Your powerful name, Jesus. Amen.

CHAPTER 12

COULD YOU NOT WATCH WITH ME?

THE ETERNAL CALL OF THE MASTER: 'STAY WITH ME'

PETER, JAMES & JOHN

GETHSEMANE: WHERE THE NIGHT SEES GOD ON HIS KNEES

If Jerusalem was asleep, Gethsemane was awake. The trees creaked softly with the wind; branches cast long shadows on the ground; the moon fell like a pale reflection over the rocks. There, in that silent garden, slow footsteps were heard, and then a sigh that did not seem human. It was Jesus.

He did not choose that place by accident. Gethsemane—"oil press"—was the place where the olive was crushed, where it was pressed between stones to release the best it carried within. There, the ordinary became precious. There, what was broken became oil.

And that night, the oil did not come from olives. It came from a heart being pressed.

The Mount of Olives already carried memory:
– David wept there when his own son betrayed him.
– There, the glory of God paused before leaving the temple.
– Zechariah prophesied that there the feet of the Messiah would stand again when He returns.

Jesus knew every story. And still, He chose that ground to kneel. While Jerusalem slept, heaven watched. The Son of the living God—trembling, sweating like blood, bending to the ground in the darkest night in history.

That garden still speaks today: true intimacy does not happen on stages of applause, but where no one is watching—except God.

And yet, that silent scene is filled with sounds humanity needs to hear. The brush of the cloak against the soil, the groans lost among the branches, the weight of breath pressing into the earth He Himself created. Every detail of that night shouts a message: God became so human that He wept—and it is there, in the darkness of our own Gethsemanes, that we can find His heart beating for us.

The Pressed Heart:
When the Divine and the Human Collide

If Gethsemane is a press, Jesus was the olive. Not out of weakness, but out of love.

He Himself said:

"My soul is exceedingly sorrowful, even to death..."
(Matthew 26:38)

What a profoundly human, vulnerable, honest statement.
The eternal Son speaking the language of pain. Here there are no thrones. No crowds. No miracles. No multiplied bread. No demons fleeing. No teachers of the law trying to trap Him.

There are only tears.
And a whisper: *"Father, if it is possible..."* *(Matthew 26:39)*

Jesus was expressing what you express when you say:
"Lord, I can't anymore."
"Lord, this is heavy."
"Lord, help me."

Gethsemane teaches us that knowing God does not spare you from agony; it accompanies you in it. Jesus was not putting on a spiritual show. He was pouring out His soul.

That is why this place is so sacred: it is the exact point where the divine chose to feel human, so that the human could draw near to the divine.

And this collision between the divine and the human was not an accidental tragedy, but the most intense manifestation of love. It was love that led Him there, not duty. It was love that kept Him there, even as the earth trembled under the weight of His decision. The press was squeezing His heart, and what came out was not despair, but a sacred blend of pain and obedience—one that would perfume the history of humanity with the fragrance of sacrifice.

THE MOST HUMAN REQUEST OF JESUS: "STAY WITH ME"

Christ could have said anything. He could have given an instruction. He could have preached. He could have taught a parable. He could have asked for a miracle from heaven.

But He didn't. He asked for something so simple, so human, so tender, that it breaks the soul:

"Watch with Me."

With Me. With My pain. With My sorrow. With My burden. With My night He did not ask: "Watch over the mission." "Watch over the Church." "Watch over the ministry."

He asked: "Can you be with Me?"

There is no more intimate phrase in the Gospels. Jesus was not looking for strong people; He was looking for present friends.

That is still His desire today. He asks for your companionship. Not your preaching. Not your agenda. Not your performance. Not your perfection.

Just your presence.

An "I'm here."

Sometimes we think intimacy with God means praying loudly, speaking beautifully, using long phrases. But Gethsemane shows us the opposite: intimacy is sitting close while He sighs.

And when He asks us to stay with Him, He is not looking for elaborate words, but for an open heart. He invites us to share in His most vulnerable moments to show us that our relationship with Him is sustained by shared love, by silent comfort, by a closeness that is not afraid to look pain in the eyes and remain there. That simple request continues to echo in our hearts: "Would you stay with Me?" And it is not a duty, but a privilege—to be companions of the Son of God when His humanity is expressed with the greatest intensity.

THE SLEEP THAT REVEALS DISTANCE: WHEN FAITH NODS OFF

We do not always fall asleep because we are physically tired. Sometimes we fall asleep because we drift away without realizing it.

The disciples were only steps away from Jesus—yet asleep.

And Jesus was only steps away from them—yet awake. Sleep is not a sin. It is a symptom. It is the soul saying: "I am overwhelmed." "I am sad." "I am saturated." "I have no strength left."

The Gospel says they were filled with sorrow. And sorrow does not only make us cry—it makes us sleep. Sometimes you fall asleep not because your body is tired, but because your heart is emotionally exhausted.

Jesus does not scold the disciples. He does not abandon them.

He does not tell them they failed as friends. He simply asks—with a tenderness that disarms:

"Could you not watch with Me one hour?"

And behind that question there is another, even softer "Do you still love Me enough to stay close?" "Do you still want to be near My heart? Because spiritual distance is not revealed by shouting. It is revealed by yawning.

Has it ever happened to you that you are physically present in spiritual spaces, but your mind and heart are far away? The disciples' sleep is a mirror of our distractions: we can be close to Jesus with our bodies, but far away with our attention.

The body sits in a church chair, but the mind is in the week's to-do list, on a phone screen, or buried in worries The heart can be asleep while we sing songs.

And Jesus, in the gentleness that defines Him, looks at us and asks that question that is diagnosis and embrace at the same time:

"Could you not watch with Me one hour?"

He is not shaming you; He is waking you up. He wants you to see that every spiritual yawn is a wake-up call—to return, to reconnect, to remember why you follow the One who poured out His life for you.

Every time your faith nods off, He touches your shoulder and whispers:

"Wake up. I am still here."

SEEK HIM WHILE HE MAY BE FOUND: THE OPPORTUNITY OF NOW

The Bible does not say, "Seek God when you feel like it." Nor does it say, "Seek Him when you are in a good season."

It says:

"Seek the LORD while He may be found..." (Isaiah 55:6)

There are windows of opportunity. Moments when the heart is softer. Moments when the Spirit whispers more closely. Moments when God says, "Come... now."

Not because He hides, but because the human heart learns to postpone its response.

Prayer gets postponed. Surrender gets postponed. Time alone with God gets postponed. Obedience to what was already clear gets postponed.

Many Christians serve God, but do not spend time with Him. Many talk about God, but no longer talk to Him. Many are close to the atmosphere, but far from intimacy.

Jesus keeps calling: "Do not leave it for tomorrow. Do not wait until you are ready. Do not wait until you are strong. Seek Me while I allow Myself to be found."

Intimacy begins with a yes—even if it is weak. Even if it is tired. Even if it comes through tears. But it begins.

Because although the grace of God is abundant, the human heart adapts. Spiritual indifference does not always appear as open sin, but as a lethargy that extinguishes first love. That is why the invitation to seek Him "while He may be found" is, at the same time, an act of divine mercy and an urgent call. God is always willing to receive us, but our timing in responding can determine how much living water we drink and how deeply it satisfies us.

In a culture of constant postponement, where everything seems delayable, Jesus interrupts with a single word: now. Not because of divine whim, but because today has a power that tomorrow does not. Today you can fall in love again. Today you can recover the sensitivity routine has stolen. Today you can hear what you once heard clearly.

Do not postpone what the Spirit is awakening in your heart. Because the window that is open in this season may not be open with the same intensity in another—not because God closes it, but because you may not have the same hunger, thirst, and desperation.

THE INNER CIRCLE: WHY ONLY PETER, JAMES, AND JOHN?

Jesus had twelve disciples, but three lived closer to His heart. At the resurrection of Jairus's daughter, He took only those three.

At the Transfiguration, only they saw His glory. In Gethsemane, only they were close enough to hear His soul tremble.

Why them? The Bible does not give an explicit reason, but it gives us clues.

1. **They were the first called**. They had been with Jesus from the very beginning.

2. **They had intense personalities:** Peter was impulsive; James and John were called "sons of thunder." Three emotional volcanoes. Three living flames that needed direction.

3. **They had distinct and crucial futures:** Peter would become the voice of the newborn church. James, the first martyr. John, the last witness.

Three different destinies, but all three needed a finely tuned heart. Jesus does not form leaders from a distance. He forms them through closeness. That is why He called them further in.

The circle of three was not an exclusive club; it was a laboratory of transformation. Jesus, the wise Master, knew that these three needed more refining, more love, more correction, more closeness. And He also knew that these three would need a heart prepared to sustain the church that would be born at Pentecost. Peter would need to remember the face of the Master who sweat blood when he himself would face martyrdom. James would have to carry with him the memory of Jesus kneeling as he faced Herod's sword. And John would need the memory of his Master's heart when he later wrote one of the most intense love statements in Scripture:

"My little children, let us not love in word or in tongue, but in deed and in truth".

(1 John 3:18)

Jesus did not give them a privilege. He gave them a weight. Being part of the inner circle was not a reward; it was a call to die more, to serve more, to love more deeply. And that is what intimacy with God means: it gives you access to His heart, but it also asks you to open yours—to be transformed and to become a purer instrument.

WHAT JESUS FORMED IN THEM... AND WHAT HE WANTS TO FORM IN YOU

Sometimes we believe that God calls us because of our abilities. But in Gethsemane something very different is revealed:

God calls by intimacy, not by talent.

Jesus wanted them to see three things:
1. **His vulnerability.** The Master wept in front of them. That image would follow them for the rest of their lives. They would never preach again without remembering that God, made man, also sweat like drops of blood.

2. **His surrender.** They heard the most dangerous prayer in the world: "...not My will, but Yours be done" (Luke 22:42). Do you want purpose? Start there. That is the sentence that opens closed doors and shuts the wrong paths.

3. **His perseverance.** Jesus went back to pray three times. Three times He knelt. Three times He spoke with His Father. He persevered in the presence to teach them that true strength does not come from avoiding pressure, but from surrendering under it.

And now He asks you: Do you want to be among the three? Do you want to be part of the circle that hears His sighs? Do you want to walk so close that you can feel His pain and His joy?

Intimacy is not inherited. It is pursued.

To form a disciple, God does not first give a map—He gives a mirror.

He wants us to see ourselves reflected in the vulnerability of Jesus and to understand that surrender is not cowardly resignation, but an act of radical trust. Perseverance is not insisting on our will, but insisting on remaining in His. Jesus brought them close so they could experience these truths firsthand. God's vulnerability before them was not an accident; it was a model.

When you draw near to God, He does not hide His humanity in Jesus. He shows you a heart that breaks over sin, that aches over unbelief, that bleeds for humanity. He shows you that true leadership is not built on platforms, but on prayer-soaked ground stained with tears. He teaches you that obedience is a renewed decision, not a passing emotion. He shows you that persevering in His presence is not monotony, but oxygen for the soul.

He wants to form in you the ability to weep with those who weep and to fight for those who cannot. He wants you to be someone who surrenders to the divine plan even when that plan includes dark nights. He wants you, like Peter, James, and John, to carry such a vivid memory of His face in agony that you could never turn ministry into a business, preaching into a performance, or worship into a routine.

WHEN GOD INVITES YOU INTO HIS HEART: REVELATION, REST, AND AN OPEN EAR

God calls many. But He opens His heart only to those who draw near.

He offers you three gifts that exist only in intimacy:
1. **Rest.** "Come to Me, all you who are weary…" It is not a mattress. It is His chest. There are wounds that are not healed by advice, but by companionship.

2. **Direction.** "I will teach you the way…" The will of God does not arrive through Google or ChatGPT. It comes in intimate conversations. It comes in whispers. It comes when you say, "Lord, speak to me… I'm staying to listen."

3. **Revelation.** "Great and hidden things…" God is not silent. He speaks. He reveals. He whispers. He warns. He promises. He entrusts secrets to those who stay awake with Him.

Intimacy is not a spiritual luxury.
It is survival for the soul.

Because revelation is not merely information; it is transformation. Discovering what God wants to say to you has the power to break chains of doubt, realign destinies, and give meaning to seasons that seem pointless. Rest is not the absence of problems; it is the presence of God in the middle of them. Direction is not a route without challenges; it is a path walked with the One who knows exactly where He is going—and why.

In a culture of productivity, where value is measured by what we do, Jesus offers you a space where value is received for who you are: His son, His daughter, His friend. There He teaches you to rest as an act of faith, instructs you in secret about crucial decisions, and reveals what is hidden—not so you can boast in knowledge, but so you can walk in obedience.

WHEN YOU'VE SEEN MIRACLES, BUT HE ASKS FOR SOMETHING ELSE: NEARNESS

Peter, James, and John had seen:

- demons cast out,

- loaves multiplied,

- the dead raised,

- storms silenced,

- a little girl open her eyes,

- the face of Jesus shining with glory.

They had witnessed what many preachers dream of seeing in an entire lifetime. And yet… on the most important night, He did not ask them to perform a miracle. He asked them to be there.

Because there is a kind of faith that is not formed by watching miracles, but by witnessing tears.

And there is a kind of calling that is not born in applause, but in silent intimacy. Jesus asks you today: Is what I can do enough for you? Or do you want to know who I am?

Do you want to stay with Me even when I am not doing anything spectacular?

That is the test of the intimate ones.
That is the depth of true callings.
That is the essence of Gethsemane.

Many times we ask for signs, wonders, and external answers, when what Jesus desires is that we remain with Him in His silences. Miracles matter—they are signs of His power—but intimacy with Him is the higher goal. When you have seen the supernatural, your faith is strengthened; but when you stay with Him without seeing, your heart becomes intertwined with His. That is where you learn to trust His character beyond His actions, to love His presence beyond His power, to value His silence as much as His thunderous voice.

Knowing Jesus is not an agenda of spectacular events, but a daily walk where the greatest revelation may be a whisper in the heart. In Gethsemane, Jesus did not perform a miracle; He wept. And in those tears, the deepest dimension of His love was revealed. Do you love Jesus only for what He does, or also for who He is when He does nothing? That question defines intimacy. The closeness He seeks is not formed in public acts, but in nights of silence and shared tears.

"COULD YOU NOT WATCH WITH ME?" APPLIED TO YOUR LIFE TODAY

Read it again. Slowly. As if Jesus were saying it to you with His hand on your shoulder:

"Could you not watch with Me?"

He is not saying: "Could you not stay awake for an entire half-night vigil?" Nor: "Could you not be perfect?" Nor: "Could you not produce more?"

He is saying:

"Could you not stay close? Could you not talk with Me? Could you not keep Me company in My heart?"

Watching with Jesus today means:

Turning down the noise to hear His voice. Removing spiritual masks. Showing Him your real exhaustion.

Telling Him the truth:

"Lord, I miss You." "Lord, I fell asleep." "Lord, wake me up."

Because your spiritual dreams are not activated by performance, but by closeness. Your calling is not ignited by talent, but by the chest where you once rested. Your promises are not fulfilled through activity, but through intimacy.

Gethsemane is not a place for the strong. It is a place for the sincere.

And this invitation must echo in your daily present.

Where are you sleeping spiritually? In what areas have you stopped being attentive to the Master's voice because busyness, routine, or even spiritual fatigue has lulled you to sleep?

This call from Jesus is not a rebuke, but a loving reminder that, in the end, the only thing that sustains your life, your ministry, your calling, your dreams, your promises, is your ability to stay awake with Him.

It is not about how many events you organize, how many campaigns you lead, how many people you impact. It is about how deeply you know His voice.How sensitive you are to His whispers.

How available you are to His silences. Watching with Him today is saying:
"I don't want to miss Your sigh because I am busy with my spiritual agenda."

It is confessing:
"I don't want more noise that silences Your song over me."

And it is embracing this truth:
"I don't want another achievement that pulls me away from Your presence." Watching is letting go of what is urgent to embrace what is truly important.

PRAYER: HERE I WANT TO WATCH WITH YOU

Lord Jesus, thank You for that garden where Your tears mingled with the soil.

Thank You for inviting me to watch with You when You Yourself were trembling.

Today I acknowledge that many times I have fallen asleep just steps away from Your presence. Sometimes because of sorrow. Sometimes because of exhaustion. Sometimes because I didn't know how to draw near But here I am. I do not come with perfect words. I come with an awakened heart. I come because I need You, and because I miss You.

Teach me to seek You while You allow Yourself to be found. Teach me to watch not out of obligation, but out of love. Let me feel Your heart. Show me Your secrets. Direct my steps. Awaken my soul.

Let me be one of those who stays with You even when my eyes grow heavy, even when my soul trembles, even when it costs me.

Let my soul learn that watching with You is the greatest honor a human being can have: the honor of knowing Your suffering and Your glory, of sharing in Your tears and Your joy, of embracing Your silence and Your songs.

Help me stop postponing intimacy with You. Help me desire Your presence more than Your gifts. Make my heart a Gethsemane where the oil of my love for You is pressed out, and where my tears mingle with Yours — not to suffer for the sake of suffering, but to share in the burden that saves us.

And when You ask me again, "Could you not watch with Me?" may my whole life answer:

"Yes, Lord. Here I am. Here I want to be. Here I will rest. Here I will watch with You, because there is nowhere else I want to be. Because with You… everything makes sense." Amen.

CHAPTER 13
WHY ARE YOU PERSECUTING ME?

I WAS SINCERELY WRONG—AND YET...

SAUL

HE WAS NOT A THIEF, HE WAS A "DEFENDER OF THE FAITH"

If this were a chapter about a repentant thief, it would be easier to read. But Saul of Tarsus was not a street criminal, nor a public adulterer, nor a corrupt tax collector.

He was a man of Scripture, of the temple, of prayer, of discipline. He was the kind of person who, in our churches today, would teach classes, lead groups, and impress us with his knowledge.

He himself tells the story years later:

> *"Indeed, I am a Jew, born in Tarsus of Cilicia, but brought up in this city at the feet of Gamaliel, taught according to the strictness of our fathers' law, and was zealous toward God..."*
>
> *(Acts 22:3)*

Tarsus was an important city in the Greco-Roman world; Jerusalem was the religious center of his people. Saul moved comfortably between both worlds: a Roman citizen, a Jewish Pharisee, a student of the greatest teacher of his time.

Later he would say that in Judaism he "advanced beyond many" of his contemporaries and that he was "extremely zealous for the traditions" of his fathers *(Galatians 1:13–14)*.

He did not begin as Paul the Apostle. He began as Saul the convinced. And that is what makes this story dangerous:

Saul was not lost in chaos. He was lost inside his religious certainty.

HE LIVED IN THE TIME OF JESUS... YET DID NOT RECOGNIZE HIM

When Stephen is stoned, Luke includes a brutal detail:
"And the witnesses laid down their clothes at the feet of a young man named Saul. And Saul was consenting to his death".

(Acts 7:58; 8:1)

Luke calls him a young man.

Jesus had died and risen only a few years earlier, and most historians place the death of Stephen and the persecution in Jerusalem around A.D. 34–36, just a few years after the crucifixion and ascension of Jesus (around A.D. 30–33).

That means Saul lived in the same generation as Jesus.

While Jesus was preaching in Galilee and Jerusalem, Saul already existed— growing, studying, being formed, filling his mind with Scripture.

Perhaps he heard rumors of a rabbi who healed the sick and ate with sinners. Perhaps he heard echoes of the cross. Perhaps he listened to debates about that Nazarene whom some called "the Son of God."

But one thing is to live in the time of Jesus, and something very different is to recognize Jesus.

Saul lived in the right era, near the right places, with the right texts— and still ended up standing on the opposite side of the risen Christ.

FROM APPLAUSE TO STONES: THE DAY THE PERSECUTION BEGAN

After Stephen's death, Acts says:

> *"On that day a great persecution arose against the church which was at Jerusalem… And Saul was ravaging the church, and entering house after house, dragging off men and women, committing them to prison".*

(Acts 8:1–3)

He was not a bystander. He was a protagonist. He entered homes. He shattered spaces of intimacy. He dragged people out by force. He sent entire families to prison.

But listen to him years later, after he had already met Christ:

> *"I indeed thought I must do many things contrary to the name of Jesus of Nazareth".*

(Acts 26:9)

Read that phrase carefully: *"I thought I must."*
He does not say, "Out of cruelty."
He does not say, "Out of pure hatred."
He says, "I believed it was my duty."

Saul did not see himself as a brutal persecutor, but as a responsible defender. He felt no remorse; he felt he was serving God.

And that is where he begins to look far too much like us.

ON THE ROAD TO DAMASCUS: ERROR DRESSED AS OBEDIENCE

The story accelerates in Acts 9:

> *"Then Saul, still breathing threats and murder against the disciples of the Lord, went to the high priest and asked letters from him to the synagogues of Damascus, so that if he found any who were of the Way, whether men or women, he might bring them bound to Jerusalem".*

> *(Acts 9:1–2)*

Look at the picture: He has religious approval. He has official letters. He has a structured plan. He goes after "those of the Way" as if he were carrying out a necessary service.

If he lived today, his calendar would be full, his inbox filled with thank-you emails, perhaps letters of recommendation from his leaders. He might be posting Bible verses while organizing the next raid "for the truth."

Saul is not the chapter of scandalous sin. He is the chapter of error dressed as obedience.

BRUTAL LIGHT AND AN AUDIBLE VOICE: THE DEAD ONE WHO SPEAKS

Then God decides to stop him on the road:

> *"But as he journeyed, it happened that he came near Damascus, and suddenly a light shone around him from heaven. Then he fell to the ground and heard a voice saying to him, 'Saul, Saul, why are you persecuting Me?'"*

> *(Acts 9:3–4)*

253

It was not an idea.
It was not a metaphor.
It was a voice.

Later, when Saul retells the story in Jerusalem, he says:
"I heard a voice saying to me…" (Acts 22:7).
And before Agrippa he insists that it was Jesus of Nazareth
Himself speaking to him from heaven (Acts 26:13–15).

The Jesus Saul considered dead, defeated, blasphemous…
that same Jesus speaks to him in an audible voice.

It was not the hallucination of a guilty fanatic. It was not the trick of disciples who stole a body. It was not a "collective vision" produced by trauma. It was a direct encounter with the **Risen One.**
And before revealing who He is, Jesus asks him a question.

WHEN GOD CALLS YOU BY NAME… TWICE

"Saul, Saul…"

In the Bible, God does not repeat names out of nervousness. Every double calling marks a before and an after:

- **"Abraham, Abraham"** – to stop a knife and reveal a ram in place of Isaac *(Genesis 22:11–12).*

- **"Moses, Moses"** – from the burning bush, to pull a fugitive out of anonymity and begin the exodus *(Exodus 3:4).*

- **"Samuel, Samuel"** – in the night, when the word was rare, to raise up a child prophet *(1 Samuel 3:10)*.

- **"Martha, Martha"** – in a house full of dishes and duties, to reorder affection and priorities *(Luke 10:41)*.

- **"Simon, Simon"** – before the denial, to announce both the sifting and the restoration *(Luke 22:31)*.

And now, on a dusty road, far from Jerusalem, the same voice from heaven says:
"Saul, Saul…"

When God repeats your name: He stops your hurry. He bypasses your excuses. He goes straight to the root of your identity. He marks an invisible boundary: up to here your path; from here on, Mine.

He does not call him "persecutor," nor "fanatic," nor "murderer."

He calls him by the name his parents once spoke with love. He speaks not to the persecutor he became, but to the man He knew

"from the womb." (Galatians 1:15)

"WHY ARE YOU PERSECUTING ME?" – WHEN JESUS TAKES IT PERSONALLY

The question is short, but devastating:
"Saul, Saul, why are you persecuting Me?" (Acts 9:4)

Saul could have answered:

"I am not persecuting You; I am persecuting those strange people."

But Jesus does not see that separation.
On another occasion He had already said:

> *"Whatever you did to one of the least of these My brothers, you did to Me".*

> *(Matthew 25:40)*

Years later, Paul would understand that the church is the "body of Christ." To touch the body is to touch the Head. To persecute the disciples is to persecute the Lord.

And here appears the most uncomfortable angle of the chapter:

Saul did not hate God. He loved his version of God so much that he ended up fighting against God Himself.

That is spiritual pride: Loving your interpretation so much that you are no longer correctable.

WHEN YOUR PRAYER CHANGES DIRECTION: "WHO ARE YOU, LORD?"

Saul does not ask:

"What is happening?" "Why this light?" "Why are You doing this to me?"

His mouth says:

"Who are You, Lord?..." (Acts 9:5)

That is the crack where grace enters. Until that day, Saul spoke about God. Now he speaks to God.

He had spent years studying the Scriptures, but he had never asked that question with humility. He had doctrine, yes. He had tradition. He had certainty. But he did not know the Son.

Until you dare to pray:
"Lord... I thought I knew You, but who are You really?"
you will keep calling "defending the faith"
things that heaven calls "persecution."

"I AM JESUS" – THE NAME SAUL DESPISED

The answer from heaven does not hesitate:

"I am Jesus, whom you are persecuting". (Acts 9:5)

He does not say: "I am the Most High, the Eternal, the Almighty...".
He says: *"Jesus"*—the name Saul associated with deception, with heresy, with a cursed crucified man.

And He adds: "whom you are persecuting." There is no room to soften it. He does not say: "You have drifted a little." He says: "You have been striking Me."
This is the surgery of the Spirit: He names the problem

without destroying you. He does not disguise your error, but He does not cancel your story either.

Behind that sentence, however, there is a decision of grace: Jesus does not crush him. He does not strike him down. He does not erase him. He confronts him in order to rescue him.

THERE IS NO MAP, ONLY THE NEXT STEP

After revealing Himself, Jesus does not hand him a five-year plan. He tells him:

> *"Arise and go into the city, and you will be told what you must do".*
>
> *(Acts 9:6)*

Nothing like: "You will be an apostle to the Gentiles." "You will write letters that generations will read." "You will preach before kings." Only: "Get up. Go in. Wait. Listen."

Spiritual pride is dismantled this way: by obeying simple instructions without demanding full explanations.

THREE DAYS BLIND: WHEN THE PAUSE IS A GIFT

The account continues:

> *"Then Saul arose from the ground, and when his eyes were opened he saw no one. But they led him by the hand and brought him into Damascus. And he was three days without sight, and neither ate nor drank".*
>
> *(Acts 9:8–9)*

The man who entered houses with authority now has to be led by the hand. The one who saw errors in everyone now sees nothing. The one who gave orders now obeys. The one who always had something to say falls silent.

It was not a capricious punishment. It was pedagogy. God detoxifies him from his way of seeing.

Three days without sight. Three days without control. Three days without "doing things for God." Only thinking. Only remembering. Only letting the Spirit dismantle his narrative: remembering Stephen's face. remembering the screams of families. remembering the words he had despised.

> *There are pauses that feel like punishment, but they are surgeries of mercy.*

GOD DOESN'T CHANGE HIS NAME; HE CHANGES HIS FOCUS

Many people preach that God "changed Saul's name" to Paul, the way He did with Abram/Abraham or Jacob/Israel. But the Bible never records such a moment.

What we do read is:

"Then Saul, who also is called Paul..."

(Acts 13:9)

Saul already had both names: one Hebrew (Saul), one Roman (Paul). What changes is not his civil record. What changes is for whom and for what he uses his story.

His Pharisaic training becomes a tool to explain Christ from the Scriptures. His Roman citizenship allows him to appeal to Caesar and reach Rome. His Greek and Jewish worlds turn him into a bridge between cultures.

God does not erase the studious, intense, passionate Saul. What He does is redirect him.

That is why this chapter is not about a "new motivational name." It is the chapter where you discover that you don't need a new nickname to receive a new heart.

MISTAKEN... AND YET CALLED

Years later, now as an apostle, Paul writes:

> *"I was formerly a blasphemer, a persecutor, and an insolent man; but I obtained mercy... Christ Jesus came into the world to save sinners, of whom I am chief".*
>
> *(1 Timothy 1:13–15)*

And also:

> *"For you have heard of my former conduct in Judaism, how I persecuted the church of God beyond measure and tried to destroy it... But when it pleased God, who separated me from my mother's womb and called me through His grace, to reveal His Son in me..."*
>
> *(Galatians 1:13–16)*

Look at the tension:

"Persecuted beyond measure."

"Tried to destroy the church."

"Blasphemer, persecutor, insolent man."

And at the same time:
"Separated from the womb."
"Called by His grace."
"Obtained mercy."

Saul is the chapter where you understand that you can be sincerely mistaken and still have been sincerely called before you were born.

The calling does not excuse the damage. But the damage does not cancel the calling.

CONSEQUENCES: A CALLING WITH UNCOMFORTABLE WITNESSES

God forgives him, but people do not forget so quickly. When he tries to join the disciples in Jerusalem:

"But they were all afraid of him, and did not believe that he was a disciple".

(*Acts 9:26*)

And later:

"Now after many days were past, the Jews plotted to kill him... then the disciples took him by night and let him down through the wall in a large basket".

(*Acts 9:23–25*)

Not everyone buys the change. Some want to kill him. Others are suspicious. Others need time.

Saul does not spend months trying to prove that he has changed. He does not launch public-relations campaigns. He simply obeys the Spirit and lets his life speak.

There are mistakes in your past that will have a long memory. People who saw your "Saul" and do not know what to do with your "Paul." Your task is not to convince everyone.

Your task is to walk hand in hand with the Spirit and let Him use your story however He chooses.

THE SAUL THAT STILL LIVES IN US (MY OWN MISSTEP)

Let me confess something to you. I've also had my own "Damascus" moments—without a heavenly light, but with a blown tire.

Some time ago at work, there was another leader at my same level. His decisions, his leadership style, the way he spoke about my team... everything started to make my blood boil. I felt our help wasn't being valued, that my people were being treated as if they were weak, as if I didn't know how to lead.

And here's the irony: inside, I thought my anger was "holy." "I'm defending my people. I'm defending what's right."

One day I snapped. I confronted him in front of others. I raised my voice. I delivered a "back off" disguised as a speech. In short, I told him: "Let me do my thing, and you do yours."

I left work convinced I was right. I got in the car with my chest puffed out and my spirit "righteously indignant."

I was so absorbed in my version of the story—telling Milka what had happened— that I almost missed my exit. I tried to merge at the last second... and fell into a holy pothole that blew my tire.

New car. No spare tire. A modern system that was supposed to seal itself... and didn't. Tow truck. Waiting. Expense. Frustration.

Was it the devil? Was it God? I'm not going to do theology with a pothole in the road. But I do know this: while I was sitting there, stuck, unable to continue my route, the Spirit began speaking to me louder than any speech I had just given.

I wasn't entirely wrong in what I saw. But I was deeply wrong in how I reacted.

I confused legitimate pain with a license to humiliate. Zeal for what was right with permission to trample. Defending my team with permission to disrespect someone else.

The next day, I apologized. The relationship didn't become perfect overnight. There were still frictions afterward.

During an emotional intelligence training, on a break, I approached him again and said something like: "I'm very emotional... but I still need a bit more emotional intelligence. Forgive me for how I spoke to you."

We hugged. We didn't erase what happened, but we opened a new door.

The Saul in me didn't show up by stoning anyone. He showed up thinking: "I'm so right that the way I act doesn't matter."

And that's when the Spirit said to me "You are sincerely wrong. And yet... I do not discard you. But I will correct you."

EVERYDAY EXAMPLES OF SPIRITUAL PRIDE
Maybe you don't go from house to house arresting Christians.

But the "inner Saul" shows up when: you believe you have the right to destroy reputations "because you're defending the truth."

You use Bible verses like stones to win family arguments. You treat your husband, wife, children, or church like projects that must adapt to your "biblical" way of seeing things—without listening to their wounds. You post attacks on social media, carefully armed with doctrine, but empty of compassion. You serve nonstop in church, but it's been a long time since you last asked Jesus:

"Did You want me to do this... or did I put myself on this agenda?"

Saul was not saved from a scandalous sin. He was saved from a spiritual pride that made him believe he was right while he was destroying others.

EVEN AFTER DAMASCUS...
YOU STILL NEED CORRECTION

That is why it is so important to connect this chapter with the next one: the Holy Spirit.

Because after Damascus, Paul does not become perfect. He remains intense. He argues so sharply with Barnabas over Mark that they end up separating *(Acts 15:36–40)*. He speaks of a "thorn in the flesh" that keeps him humble *(2 Corinthians 12:7–9)*.

In other words: the redirection on the road to Damascus did not turn him into a plaster statue. It turned him into a man dependent on the Spirit. The same is true for you. Maybe you already had your Damascus. You already had your fall. You already had your moment of: "I was the one who was wrong."

Even so, you still need: to be filled with the Spirit. to be guided by the Spirit. to be corrected by the Spirit.

This chapter does not end with "Here I am, send me." That phrase does not belong to Saul. What belongs to Saul is this:

> *"I was sincerely wrong, and yet God called me.*
> *Now I need the Spirit so I don't return to the same pride wearing a different suit."*

QUESTIONS TO KEEP YOU
ON THE GROUND A LITTLE LONGER

Before you pray, let me leave you with a few questions—no decoration, no polish:

- In what area of your life are you convinced, yet the Spirit has been unsettling you for a long time?

- Whom have you wounded "for defending what's right"? Specific names. Specific faces.

- What recent interruption (an illness, an argument, a failure, a forced pause) might be the equivalent of your Damascus light?

- If Jesus said to you today: "_____, _____, why are you persecuting Me?" what would He be pointing to?

Would you dare to pray again the kind of prayer that tastes less like success and more like surrender:

"Who are You, Lord... and what do You want me to do?"

Don't answer too fast. Stay on the ground a little longer. Let the Spirit show you where you have been sincerely wrong—and yet, sincerely called.

PRAYER:
"Do Not Let Me Keep Running the Wrong Way"

Lord Jesus,
You who called Saul by his name—twice—you know me more
deeply than I know myself.

I confess that there are areas where I feel convinced, yet I may
be sincerely mistaken.

I do not want to love my version of You more than You Yourself.
If You need to interrupt my agenda, my character, my "way of
doing things," do it.

Do not discard me, but do not leave me unchanged.
Tear down my spiritual pride.
Show me whom I have hurt while believing I was defending You.
Give me the courage to ask for forgiveness and the humility to
let myself be led by the hand.

Thank You because, just as with Saul, You can take my error,
my story, my difficult character, and redirect it.

Teach me to live each day asking:
"Who are You, Lord?
What do You want me to do?"

And may the Holy Spirit, in the next step, be the One who
corrects, guides, and sustains what You began on my own road
to Damascus.

Amen.

CHAPTER 14
DID YOU RECEIVE THE HOLY SPIRIT?

SECTION I: WHEN YOU DISCOVER THAT THE AUTHOR OF YOUR STORY LIVES WITHIN YOU

HOLY SPIRIT

NOT A LESSON…
BUT A LIVING STORY

This chapter is not meant to be a formal class about the person of the Holy Spirit. You will not find here a course in systematic theology, nor a seminary-style lecture with whiteboards, charts, and Greek terms. This chapter is, above all, a testimony. It is an honest conversation from someone who has stumbled, searched, doubted, insisted, wept… and has been patiently guided by the most misunderstood—and at the same time, most necessary—Person in all of Christian life: the Holy Spirit.

The book of Acts records a very particular encounter between the apostle Paul and some disciples in Ephesus. Scripture says:

> *"And it happened, while Apollos was at Corinth, that Paul, having passed through the upper regions, came to Ephesus. And finding some disciples he said to them, 'Did you receive the Holy Spirit when you believed?' So they said to him, 'We have not so much as heard whether there is a Holy Spirit.'"*
>
> *(Acts 19:1–2)*

That response is surprising—and at the same time, deeply current. It summarizes the reality of many believers today: good, sincere people who love Jesus, yet live with little awareness that the Holy Spirit exists, that He is a Person, that He desires relationship with them, and that He longs to transform their lives from the inside out.

Notice that Paul did not ask them to take a theology exam. He did not ask whether they understood complex doctrines about the nature of Christ, nor whether they knew technical terms about the Holy Spirit. His question was simple and profound:

"Did you receive the Holy Spirit when you believed?" In other words: is this only information in your head, or is it a reality within you?

There is an enormous difference between knowing a concept and knowing the Holy Spirit; between knowing that He exists and living as if He truly dwells within you. That is the heart of this chapter.

A BURNING DESIRE THAT COLLIDED WITH THE REALITY OF GRACE

When I was reconciled with God, a fierce desire to know the Holy Spirit was ignited within me. It was not theoretical curiosity. It was not a casual "how interesting this thing about the Spirit is." It was hunger. Hunger for truth. I wanted to know Him, hear Him, feel His guidance. I did not want to know about Him; I wanted to know Him.

But I was young in the faith—full of passion and short on maturity. And when you are hungry but lack spiritual discernment, you do very sincere things… and sometimes very clumsy ones. I came to believe that if I cried louder, fasted more days, wept more dramatically, trembled more intensely at the altar, then the Spirit would "come" with greater power. I thought the intensity of my actions would determine the intensity of His presence. Deep down, I was treating Him like a kind of "spiritual mechanism": if I pulled the right levers, He was obligated to manifest.

Over time, God dismantled that idea. I discovered something that changed my relationship with Him: the Holy Spirit does not respond to human pressure; He responds to surrendered hearts. He is not manipulated by my efforts; He is poured out over my surrender. He does not come because I make a lot of noise; He manifests where there is humility and faith.

I learned—sometimes the hard way—that I do not push Him; He guides me. I do not drag Him; He draws me. I do not manipulate Him; He forms me. I do not force Him; He melts me. God used many tools to teach me this: His Word; moments of correction that hurt but matured me; people who served as mirrors; and, above all, the gentle voice of the Spirit Himself— persistent, clear, and loving.

I read many books about the Holy Spirit. Some excellent, some average, and a few better left unrecommended. But even so, I discovered something incredibly valuable: books are good; seminars are useful; sermons help. But if you have the Bible and you have the Holy Spirit, you have what is essential to know Him. The main Book is in your hands.

The main Author lives inside you.

GOD SPEAKS… EVEN WHEN THERE IS NO THUNDER

We live in a culture obsessed with the spectacular. We are fascinated by dramatic testimonies: "the room shook," "the walls vibrated," "a voice thundered from heaven." We love stories where the bed moves, the curtains open by themselves, and the serial numbers on a ceiling fan feel like a prophetic code. And God, who is sovereign, can manifest Himself however He chooses. I do not limit Him.

But let me confess something with complete honesty: I have never heard the audible voice of God. I have never heard thunder calling my name. I have never seen letters floating in the air. And yet, if I were to sit down and tell you my story, I would have to say that God has spoken to me... a lot. He has guided me, corrected me, confronted me, comforted me, surprised me, and given me ideas I never would have had on my own. He has spoken so much that, at times, I have been tempted to say—half joking, half serious—"Lord... what if today You don't correct anything? Just one day off, at least?"

So how does God speak? Without turning this into a technical manual, but grounded in Scripture and in what I have lived, I would say that God speaks in many ways. He speaks first and foremost through His written Word: a phrase you have read a thousand times that suddenly pierces you like a sword; a passage that lights up precisely when you need it most. He speaks through inner impressions: that gentle but firm conviction that tells you, "this way, yes," or, "not that way." He speaks through other people: a conversation, a correction, a piece of advice that arrives at exactly the right moment. He speaks through circumstances that close one door or open another. And sometimes He speaks through a single line, a title, a song, a sermon that remains tattooed on your spirit long after the service is over.

Behind all these ways of communicating is the work of the Holy Spirit, who takes things that seem completely natural and suddenly ignites them with the light of the supernatural. He is the interpreter of the Father's voice. He is the One who translates into the language of your heart what the Father is saying.

THE DAY THE WORD "STILL" CHANGED MY CHAPTER

I want to tell you calmly about one of those moments when His voice was not audible, but it was impossible to ignore. I was finishing the book about Nicolás. It was the last chapter. I had stories, letters from Amparo and from the children, memories, tears, laughter, dates, details. But something was missing. I did not want a generic closing. I did not want just a nice sentence. I felt the book needed a seal, a word that would summarize the legacy of that man of God.

That morning I prayed something very simple, but very honest:

"Lord, something is missing. I don't want to close this book with a human ending. What is the seal of this legacy? What phrase describes what You are still doing through Nicolás's life?"

After praying, I opened a sermon online. It was not even the full message—just a fragment. The preacher began by saying a phrase that, on the surface, had nothing to do with me:

"Chapter eight... still..."

On paper, they were just words. But inside me, it was something else. The word still lit up in my spirit as if someone had underlined it with a fluorescent marker. It did not sound like coincidence; it sounded like an answer. It was not "still don't write it."

It was not "still something is missing."

It was a still full of continuity, promise, and presence. In that still, I felt the Spirit whisper to me:

"Still I am working. Still I use this life to touch generations. Still this legacy is producing fruit. Still do not close the book... because I am still writing."

That still changed the angle of the chapter, but it also changed something in me. It reminded me that the Holy Spirit does not only record the past; He extends the legacy into the future. He helped me close the book declaring that the legacy of a man of God does not end when the last page is finished, because the true Author is still writing in the children, the grandchildren, the disciples, the churches.

There was no special light in the room. There was no voice thundering from the ceiling. But in the deepest part of my spirit, I know it was Him.

THE HOLY SPIRIT AS AUTHOR AND GHOSTWRITER

In the publishing world there is an interesting figure: the ghostwriter—the writer who takes your story and puts it into words filled with grace. There are people who have incredibly rich lives, full of experiences, pain, victories, and lessons, but they do not know how to put all of that into words. So they look for someone who listens, who asks questions, who organizes, who gives shape, who finds the tone, the rhythm, the focus. The protagonist provides the life; the writer provides the pen.

That figure of the author and ghostwriter is one of the best ways I have found to describe what the Holy Spirit does in us. You have a story: childhood, wounds, decisions, mistakes, successes, moments of faith, seasons of dryness. You have pages you like and others you would rather tear out. You have chapters you would read out loud and others you would never dare to mention. The Holy Spirit enters there, into your own book, and sits beside you as the true Author.

You say, "I had a failure."

He responds, "You had a school of grace."

You think, "This part of my life is an embarrassment; it's better to rip out that page."

He whispers, "Don't tear anything out. Let Me show you how I will turn this into testimony."

You conclude, "It's over; everything ends here."

He looks at you patiently and says, "We're only on chapter three. Slow down."

The Holy Spirit does not only help you tell your story to others; He helps you tell it correctly to yourself. Because if you become your own narrator without the Spirit's help, you end up repeating lines God never wrote. You begin narrating your life with the enemy's voice: "you failed, therefore you are a failure"; "God is done with you"; "your calling was before that sin, not after"; "what you did disqualified you forever." But when the Spirit takes the pen, He writes something else over the very same scene. He does not deny what happened; He redeems it. He does not erase the pain; He redefines it. He does not hide the fall; He shows you the hand that lifted you up.

WHEN THE SPIRIT CHANGES YOUR LENSES

There is a passage in 1 Corinthians that fits perfectly with all of this. Paul, writing to a church full of gifts—but also full of confusion—speaks to them about a wisdom that does not come from human effort, but from the revelation of the Spirit. He reminds them of something written in the ancient Scriptures:

> *"Eye has not seen, nor ear heard, nor have entered into the heart of man the things which God has prepared for those who love Him. But God has revealed them to us through His Spirit. For the Spirit searches all things, yes, the deep things of God".*
>
> *(1 Corinthians 2:9–10)*

Many times we use this verse to talk about heaven, about future things, about streets of gold. And of course, it can be applied that way. But in the context of the letter, Paul is speaking about something that begins here and now: the ability to understand the wisdom of God in the middle of everyday life.

A little further on, he describes the problem of trying to understand the things of God using only human resources. He says:

> *"But the natural man does not receive the things of the Spirit of God, for they are foolishness to him; nor can he know them, because they are spiritually discerned".*
>
> *(1 Corinthians 2:14)*

Translated into everyday language, Paul is telling us this: your senses are not enough to interpret your life. Your emotions are not reliable judges of what God is doing. Your traumas are poor commentators on His character. If you look at your story only through the lenses of logic, pain, or comparison with others, you will misread it.

Without the help of the Holy Spirit, what hurts you call

punishment, when in reality it may be discipline that is saving you. What closes, you call rejection, when it may be protection. What delays, you call abandonment, when it may be preparation. And so you begin filling your book with wrong conclusions.

With the Holy Spirit, however, you begin to see what "eye has not seen." You begin to hear what "ear has not heard." You begin to embrace promises and paths that had not even entered your heart. He shows you lines you could not see before. He teaches you how to read your story from heaven's perspective.

That is why Paul can end that section with such a bold statement:

> *"For who has known the mind of the Lord that he may instruct Him? But we have the mind of Christ".*
>
> *(1 Corinthians 2:16)*

He does not say, "we have Saul's mind, upgraded to a Christian version." No. He says, "we have the mind of Christ." That is the work of the Holy Spirit. He is the One who teaches you to think like Jesus about your past, your present, your future, your calling, your wounds, and your limitations. He does not only want to change what you feel; He wants to renew the way you think.

Section II
ARE YOU WALKING IN HIS FULLNESS?

When the Spirit Becomes Your Discipline, Your Strength, and Your Warfare

When I Wanted to Pressure the Spirit... and He Wanted to Form My Character

If I'm honest, for a long time I confused emotional intensity with spiritual maturity. I thought that if I felt more, I was more filled; if I cried more, God was closer; if I shouted louder in the service, the Spirit would move more powerfully. I lived chasing intense moments, emotional highs, strong sensations. And, interestingly enough, those moments can be genuine and beautiful. But the Holy Spirit had to teach me something we don't always want to hear: He is not a special effect; He is a Person. And He came to form character, not just to provoke sensations.

In 1 Corinthians 3, Paul speaks with a mixture of love and firmness to believers who had spectacular gifts but immature character. He says:

> *"And I, brethren, could not speak to you as to spiritual people but as to carnal, as to babes in Christ. I fed you with milk and not with solid food; for until now you were not able to receive it, and even now you are still not able".*

> *(1 Corinthians 3:1–2)*

It's strong. It's as if he were saying, "You have deep experiences, but you still react like children." You can speak in tongues and still be carnal in your decisions. You can cry at the altar and still be immature in your character. You can "feel a lot" in a service and still not allow the Holy Spirit to govern what you think on Monday.

A little later, Paul asks a question that shattered many of my assumptions:

> "Do you not know that you are the temple of God and that the Spirit of God dwells in you?"
>
> (1 Corinthians 3:16)

In practice, I treated the Spirit as if He lived on the church platform: "He moves here," "He falls here," "He's strong here." I imagined Him going up and down depending on the atmosphere, the music, or the preacher. And this truth exploded inside me: the temple is not the platform; it is you. It's not that He comes down for two hours on Sunday; it's that He lives in you on Monday at 5:30 in the morning when the alarm goes off. He is there when you're sleepy, when you don't feel like it, when no one sees you, when no one applauds you.

The Holy Spirit did not come only to give you goosebumps, make you cry beautifully, or give you intense retreat experiences. He came to form the character of Christ in you: to shape the way you think, correct the way you love, cleanse the way you speak, and align the way you make decisions. He came to mature you. And that, many times, hurts more than a good tear during worship—but it produces fruit that remains.

MY DAILY RULE: I DON'T TOUCH MY PHONE UNTIL I TOUCH HEAVEN

When I understood that the Holy Spirit does not visit from time to time, but actually dwells in me, I felt there was something very practical I needed to change: the order of my mornings. I realized that my first actions of the day set the spiritual tone for everything that follows. The first nourishment your soul receives in the morning largely determines how it will breathe the rest of the day.

So I established a personal rule—simple, but radical for me: I do nothing before I pray. I don't touch my phone, my tablet, my messages, or social media until I've spoken with Him. Knees first, screens later. I'm not sharing this as a law everyone must follow, nor as a spiritual badge to show off; I share it as a testimony of something that changed my relationship with the Spirit.

I discovered that if my first breath of the day is social media, my soul wakes up tight and comparing itself. If my first breath is email, my mind starts anxious, already in urgency mode. If my first breath is the news, my heart begins worried, carrying the weight of the world. But when my first breath is something as simple as, "Holy Spirit, here I am. Direct this day. Govern my thoughts. Open the Word. Correct what needs correcting. Strengthen me where You know I am weak," the problems don't disappear—but I enter the day with the Author inside me, not the critic outside me.

It's almost funny to admit that my flesh wants to grab the phone and say, "Good morning, anxiety—where did we leave off yesterday?" Meanwhile, the Holy Spirit invites me to say, "Good morning, Lord. What are we writing today?" Such a simple phrase, repeated first thing in the morning, has become a key. It's not magic. It's not superstition. It's a daily way of reminding my soul who lives in me—and who holds the pen of my story.

WHEN THE SPIRIT TELLS YOU: "DON'T DELETE THAT CHAPTER"

Throughout this book, we've been moving chapter by chapter, question by question, life by life. There have been moments when I myself have looked at the table of contents and thought, "This chapter feels a lot like that one... what if I delete it so it's not repetitive? What if I cut here? What if I save some pages?" My editorial side raises its hand and whispers, "Tighten it. Cut it. Organize it. Be efficient."

But many times, right in the middle of that impulse to trim things down, the Holy Spirit has been very clear with me: "Don't delete it. You're not going to say the same thing. You're going to touch the same theme from another wound, from another angle, from another heart." And He was right. Theme after theme—fear, doubt, rejection, calling, shame—the Lord has shown different shades: a struggling father, a waiting woman, a fleeing prophet, a sinking disciple, a persecutor brought down by grace. Each chapter repeats God's faithfulness, but through different wounds.

I learned something very practical—not just for writing a book, but for living life: what you call repetition is often God reinforcing something you didn't fully understand the first time. The Holy Spirit is not an editor who cuts your story to make it fit fewer pages; He is a wise Author who knows exactly how many chapters you need on the same subject before the chains finally fall off. If it feels like you keep coming back to the same issue with Him, don't think it's a waste of time. It's patient grace, working in depth.

SPIRITUAL WARFARE: WHEN WRITING A CHAPTER WAKES UP HELL

If the Holy Spirit is real, the spiritual world is real as well. Not everything that happens is psychological. Not everything is simply "because you're tired" or "because you worked yourself up." There are moments when, by opening your mouth, by writing a page, by declaring a truth, you step into territory the enemy believes belongs to him. And, logically, he responds.

Let me tell you about one of those moments. While I was writing the chapter **"What Do You Want Me to Do for You?"**— where I speak deeply about Christian, about his story, his calling, and how even with his physical and sensory limitations God still has purpose and assignment for his life— we sensed that we weren't just putting together a nice chapter. We were breaking a very strong lie: the subtle but cruel idea that if someone has limitations, their calling is reduced or canceled.

As I wrote, the Spirit was confronting me and comforting me at the same time. He brought back to my memory all the doubts we had carried as parents, all the moments when, from a human perspective, Christian's future seemed "limited." And at the same time, I felt a very clear message rise in my spirit: "I do not call the way the system calls. I do not depend on diagnoses. My calling does not come with subtitles that say 'except if you have this or that.'"

We finished that chapter. And that very night, at two in the morning, Christian called me on a video call, visibly shaken:

"Daddy, I felt footsteps. Someone moved my blankets. They're knocking hard on the door…" These were visible, tangible, physical attacks. We could feel that the spiritual atmosphere was stirred. Milka and I got up, prayed, rebuked, covered the house, covered Christian, covered our minds and our emotions. And we understood something very clearly: this book is not a literary hobby. It is a declaration of war against spiritual lies.

That is why you need the Holy Spirit—not only to write chapters, but to fight battles your eyes cannot see. He is the One who wakes you up, alerts you, strengthens you, and reminds you that you are not fighting alone.

THE ARMOR DOES NOT COME WITHOUT THE PRESENCE

When we talk about spiritual warfare, it is inevitable to remember what Paul wrote to the Ephesians about the armor of God. Scripture says:

> "Finally, my brethren, be strong in the Lord and in the power of His might. Put on the whole armor of God, that you may be able to stand against the wiles of the devil. For we do not wrestle against flesh and blood, but against principalities, against powers, against the rulers of the darkness of this age, against spiritual hosts of wickedness in the heavenly places".
>
> (Ephesians 6:10–12)

Then he describes each piece:

> "Stand therefore, having girded your waist with truth, having put on the breastplate of righteousness,

and having shod your feet with the preparation of the gospel of peace; above all, taking the shield of faith with which you will be able to quench all the fiery darts of the wicked one.

And take the helmet of salvation, and the sword of the Spirit, which is the word of God; praying always with all prayer and supplication in the Spirit, being watchful to this end with all perseverance..."

(Ephesians 6:14–18)

If you want, next I can help you develop the reflection that ties this passage to your main idea—that the armor only works when it is worn in the presence of the Spirit, not as a technique but as a relationship.

It may sound like Roman armor, but it is lived out in the kitchen, at work, in the office, in the hospital, in the early morning hours when the phone rings and the news is not what you were hoping for. You and I cannot live out our calling, walk in obedience, or face attacks if we are not filled with the Holy Spirit.

The truth that girds your waist is not just doctrine; it is a Person who reminds you who you are when the enemy tries to confuse you. The breastplate of righteousness is not just a concept; it is the righteousness of Christ applied by the Spirit to your guilty heart. The shield of faith becomes very heavy if you try to lift it without the strength He gives. The sword, which is the Word, remains dead letter if the Spirit does not breathe on it and make it living and effective.

Let's be honest: at the first criticism, we want to quit. At the first closed door, we think we have no calling. At the first attack against our children, we want to run. The Holy Spirit is the One who reminds you, like a faithful ghostwriter: "This is not the end. This is a hard chapter. But the book already has an ending written: Christ wins." And He is also the One who gives you the strength to keep writing—and to keep fighting.

"DID YOU RECEIVE THE HOLY SPIRIT...?"
AND THE QUESTION OF FULLNESS

Let's return to that scene in Acts. Paul asks, "Did you receive the Holy Spirit when you believed?" They answer, "We have not so much as heard whether there is a Holy Spirit." After explaining, Paul prays for them, and the Spirit comes upon their lives in a visible way.

Today, many could give a similar answer, but with a different nuance: "I've heard of Him, but I haven't known Him"; "I've heard testimonies, but I don't have my own story with Him"; "I've heard that He moves, but I don't know what that looks like in my daily life." That's why it's important to say this clearly: if you have received Christ as your Lord and Savior, the Holy Spirit dwells in you. You don't have to bring God up and down like an elevator. It's not that He's here today, gone tomorrow, and who knows the next day. He came to dwell, not to stay as a temporary guest.

However, the question is no longer only, "Did you receive Him when you believed?" The question that now echoes is, "Are you allowing yourself to be filled by Him every day?" One thing is for His presence to be in you; something very different is for Him to rule over you. One thing is to have the Spirit; another is to walk according to the Spirit. There is a difference between carrying Him as a silent guest and recognizing Him as the host of the house.

Fullness is not a static state that happened once and that's it; it is a daily relationship, a continual "yes," a place you give Him in every area of your life.

BREAKING THE MYSTICISM: THE SPIRIT IS NOT AN EVENT

We need to tear down some strange ideas that, sometimes without realizing it, have slipped into our churches. We say things like, "Today the Holy Spirit really moved," as if yesterday He were on vacation. We comment, "The anointing was strong today," and deep down what we're measuring is how many people fell, how many shouted, how many tears we saw. And without denying that God can manifest His power in a gathering, it is dangerous to reduce the work of the Spirit to a specific moment in the church program.

It is far more powerful to be a Christian who has never fallen to the floor but lives in obedience to the Spirit from Monday to Sunday, than one who falls every week and keeps ignoring His voice at home, at the office, in marriage, in the way they treat their children. The Holy Spirit is not only the One who "makes things happen" in a service. He is the One who whispers to you in the supermarket, "Call your mom." He is the One who stops you before you send that message full of anger. He is the One who brings a verse to your mind right when you are about to give in to temptation. He is the One who wakes you in the middle of the night with a name on your heart so you will pray.

Don't wait for the next special event to feel accompanied. Don't wait for the next retreat to feel guided. Don't wait for the next prophet to receive direction. The same Spirit who guided the apostles dwells in you. That's not cheap motivation; that's Scripture. And if He lives in you, your life is no longer reduced to a series of "powerful moments"; it becomes a daily walk with Someone who never leaves you.

A SMALL PRAYER FOR BIG MOMENTS

I want to give you something very simple that I myself am practicing. It's not a magic formula, it's not a mantra, and it does not replace deep prayer or the reading of the Word.

It is simply a way to align the heart in the middle of the chaos of the day. When I feel weighed down, overwhelmed, or scattered—when my mind feels like a neighborhood full of disordered thoughts—I pray something like this:

"Holy Spirit, I breathe You in. You are in me. Give me Your sudden strength. Fill me with Your complete peace."

Sometimes I pray it before walking into a difficult meeting, before responding to a message that could hurt someone, before starting a heavy shift, before continuing to write a chapter that touches deep places. Why **"sudden strength"**? Because there are moments in life when you don't have three days to go up to the mountain, or three hours for a personal retreat. There are decisions you have to make in five minutes, with your heart racing, your mind saturated, and your phone ringing.

And in those moments, the Spirit is not only the One who strengthens you through long processes; He is also the One who gives you **sudden strength** to do what is right now.

And I ask for **"complete peace"** because you don't just need strength to do things; you need peace to avoid doing foolish things. Strength helps you move; peace helps you not move in the wrong direction. That short prayer, repeated in faith in the middle of the noise, becomes like a deep breath of the soul—a reminder that you are not alone and that, even there, the **Author** is still writing.

THE HOLY SPIRIT AND YOUR CREATIVE CALLING

If you have read this entire book, you may have noticed a certain creativity in the titles, in the structure of the chapters, in the way biblical characters are woven into our own story. Sometimes people have told me, "You're so creative—what a way to tie everything together." And if I'm honest with you, I'm not as creative as it may seem. What I do have is a creative Spirit who lives in me.

The same Spirit who moved over the surface of the waters in Genesis, the Spirit who filled Bezalel with wisdom to design the tabernacle, the Spirit who inspired psalms, parables, letters, and the great works of God throughout history, is the One who today inspires songs, business ideas, strategies for the home, new ways of relating to our children. And yes, He is the One who gives ideas for writing. He distributes gifts, talents, and callings as He wills. He breathes creativity where there was once only routine.

That is why, when I think about this book, it is not about saying, "How brilliant Saul is." It is about recognizing, "How patient, how generous, how persistent the Holy Spirit has been with Saul." He is the One who corrects, who brings focus, who cuts paragraphs that do not belong, who adds sentences that were missing, who illuminates connections I never would have seen. He is the invisible Author who takes the time to sit with me and help me put on paper what He Himself has been writing in my heart.

THE SPIRIT AND YOUR MISTAKES: DON'T STAY IN THE WRONG CHAPTER

Let's think for a moment about Peter. There was a painful chapter in his story: the night he denied Jesus three times. He had followed Him, had promised faithfulness, and yet, standing by a courtyard fire, he said again and again, "I do not know Him." The Gospel says that when the rooster crowed, Jesus looked at Peter, and Peter *"went out and wept bitterly"* *(Luke 22:61–62)*. That chapter exists. It is not erased. It is not denied.

But thanks to the Holy Spirit, it was not the final chapter.

Then came restoration. By the shore of the sea, Jesus met Peter again and, through questions that healed more than they accused, restored his calling (John 21:15–19). He did not leave him trapped in his failure; He put him back on the path. Three questions, three answers, and three commissions—different in form, but with one purpose: to restore a man so he could keep shepherding.

And then came Pentecost.
The same Peter, now filled with the Holy Spirit, stood up and spoke with boldness:

"Then Peter, standing up with the eleven, raised his voice and said to them..."

(Acts 2:14)

The result was astonishing:

"Then those who gladly received his word were baptized; and that day about three thousand souls were added to them".

(Acts 2:41)

The Spirit did not change Peter's past, but He completely transformed his future.

Do you see what the Holy Spirit does? He does not leave you stuck in your worst chapter. He does not tear out the page, but neither does He condemn you to live in it forever. He is the ultimate page-turner. He comes close and says, "Yes, that happened. Yes, it hurt. But don't close the book there. **There is still more to be written."**

So...
HAVE YOU RECEIVED THE HOLY SPIRIT?

Let's return—now for real—to the question that gives the previous section its title: *"Did you receive the Holy Spirit when you believed?"*

Maybe your answer sounds something like this: "Yes, I received Him, but I hardly talk to Him." "Yes, I received Him, but I live as if I were alone." "Yes, I received Him, but I still interpret my story through the same old lenses." If that's the case, these pages are not here to condemn you or to tell you that you're a bad Christian. They are an invitation.

They are an invitation to cultivate a relationship with Him, to surrender your desires, your agendas, your distractions, to align your day with His presence. It is an invitation to allow Him to be the **Author of your story,** not the harsh critic you invented in your own mind. To let Him teach you how to read your own life through the eyes of Christ.

And if your honest answer is, "I'm not sure... I've never thought about Him that way," then this chapter is a doorway. You do not need a spectacular mystical experience with lights, smoke, and special effects. You need to open your heart and say, with sincere faith, something as simple as this: "Jesus, I believe in You. I receive You as my Lord and Savior. And I receive the Holy Spirit, the gift You promised. Holy Spirit, dwell in me. Guide me. Correct me. Comfort me. Teach me to know Jesus." And then, each day, as you walk with Him, remind yourself that you are not alone, that you are not an orphan, that there is Someone within you who never gets tired of walking with you.

WELCOME TO A LIFE WRITTEN FROM THE INSIDE

If you've made it this far, you've already realized something important: this is not a neutral chapter. It's not just another chapter in the table of contents. This is the place where we recognize that everything else makes sense because **He** is in the middle. All the "Is there anyone...?" we've seen throughout the book—Abraham, Joseph, Moses, Joshua, Elijah, Martha, the woman with the issue of blood, Peter, Saul of Tarsus—stand firm because the same Spirit who was at work in their stories is the One at work in yours.

I don't know which part of your life's book you're in today. It may be a chapter of pain or confusion, a chapter of coming back home, of waiting, or even a chapter of victory you're still struggling to believe. What I do know is this: if the Holy Spirit lives in you, the story does not end in defeat. There may be wrinkled pages, crossed-out paragraphs, dried tears between the lines, conversations that still hurt to remember. But the **Author in the shadows** has not let go of the pen.

He keeps writing while you sleep. He keeps weaving together things you don't yet understand. He keeps using people, places, timing, and processes to give you a story that, in the end, reflects the glory of Jesus.

Welcome to a life written from the inside.

CLOSE YOUR EYES... AND BREATHE

Let me finish in a very simple way. Right where you are, if you can, close your eyes for a moment. Breathe deeply. Feel the air as it comes in and goes out. And as you do, say to the Lord, in your own words, something like this:

"Holy Spirit... I breathe You in.
You are in me.
Thank You because I do not write alone.
Thank You because I do not fight alone.
Thank You because I do not heal alone.
Thank You because I do not walk alone.
I surrender my story to You — my chapters, my wounds.
Teach me to see You on every page.
And when I want to close the book,
remind me that we are only halfway through. Amen."

And now, from the depths of my heart, I can ask you once again: **Have you received the Holy Spirit?**

If the answer is yes, live as a temple, not as a tourist.

If the answer is "I'm not sure," let this be the beginning of the most important chapter of your story: the day you discovered that **the Author of your life decided to live inside.**

CHAPTER 15
IS THERE ANYONE?

THE CALL COMES WHEN
YOU BELIEVE YOU ARE NOT READY

WHEN THE STORY RETURNS TO THE BEGINNING, BUT YOU ARE NO LONGER THE SAME

I have walked through these pages with you. One by one. Chapter after chapter. Question after question. Interruption after interruption. Sometimes we moved forward with steady steps; other times, dragging our feet. I remembered my own fears, your silences, our inner conversations. And even though we never said it out loud, we both knew this chapter was inevitable. Because every question God asks is, at its core, a disguised invitation.

He did not ask you, *"Why did you doubt?"* to shame you. He did not ask, *"What do you want Me to do for you?"* to examine your faith. He did not ask, *"Who touched Me?"* to expose your fragility. He asked in order to call you. It is as if God had been preparing us all along, tearing down excuses until reaching this moment: the moment when our response is no longer intellectual, but existential.

Now, here we are. At the point where there is no longer a need to keep explaining what He can do. This chapter is not theory. It is decision. It is that instant between the breath and the next step. If you have made it this far, it is because—even if you do not admit it—your soul is saying: "God... if You still want to use me, here I am."

This is the point where theology becomes breathing; where faith becomes movement; where the whisper of God becomes a command you can no longer ignore. Here I am is not a collection of loose words. It is an internal earthquake. It is the realization that life no longer belongs only to our plans.

I HAVE DISCOVERED SOMETHING — GOD CALLED ME WHILE I WAS SLEEPING

Let me speak to you in the first person, because before being an author, I am a disciple. I too have my internal battles, my uncomfortable silences, my nights when the pillow knows more about me than my own spirit does. And it was there, in the darkness of my doubts, that I understood something that changed everything:

God called me when I was not ready. He interrupted me when I was not searching. He spoke to me while I was distracted. He woke me up when I had already given up on myself. He did not wait for me to have a ministry, a title, a "worthy" biography. He called me when I still smelled of sea and fear, like Peter. When I was carrying history, like Joseph in the prison of Egypt. When remorse shook me like Saul on the road to Damascus.

And that lifted a weight off my shoulders. Because if He called me while I was sleeping, then He does not need me to be perfect in order to send me. He only needs me to wake up.

I see it in the story of Joseph, that young man who lay down to sleep with dreams no one understood, while God was preparing the road to Egypt and beyond *(Genesis 37; 39–41)*. I see it in Elijah, exhausted in a cave, being awakened by a whisper of the divine presence *(1 Kings 19:9–13)*. I see it in Bartimaeus, sitting by the roadside, until one day the noise of a crowd and the name of Jesus awakened him through cries of faith *(Mark 10:46–52)*. And I see it in myself, when I thought my mistakes were stronger than my calling.

"Behold, my beloved speaks and says to me: 'Arise, my love, my beautiful one, and come away.'"

(Song of Songs 2:10)

It was not an angel, it was not a prophet: it was God breaking spiritual sluggishness to bring me into a new place.

If He called me while I was sleeping, He will not leave me in the comfort of an anesthetized spirituality. This voice that interrupts is love that refuses to accept my misery as my destiny.

TODAY — NOT LATER — IS THE DAY TO RESPOND

I'm going to tell you something that took me years to admit: the excuse "when I resolve this" never ends. There is always a "when." When I heal. When I improve. When I have time. When I have strength. When everything fits. When the children grow up. When the debt is paid. When the ministry is recognized. When I finally feel like I am enough.

But God has never been a God of "when." **He is a God of "now."**

When Jesus said to Matthew, *"Follow Me"* (Matthew 9:9), He did not say:

"Follow Me when you have your accounts in order."

- When the Spirit was poured out at Pentecost, He did not wait for the disciples to have a perfect plan *(Acts 2:1–4)*.

- When the angel said to Gideon, "Go in this might of yours," he did not wait for Gideon to feel brave (*Judges 6:14*).

That is why, when I heard in my spirit that whisper I could not ignore — that "you are here, get up" — I knew it was not a biblical poem. It was an ultimatum of love. The moment was not later. The moment was that very second. And I sense the same thing for you. Maybe you were waiting for a few more months of "preparation." God says: "Do not postpone it. Respond now."

It is not a plea for tomorrow; it is a plea for today. To present your body as a living sacrifice does not mean waiting for perfection, but offering yourself just as you are.

IF GOD BROUGHT YOU THIS FAR, IT WAS NOT TO MAKE YOU A SPECTATOR

I want you to understand this: God does not invest questions in someone without purpose. He does not sow confrontation in barren soil. He would not have kept asking you if His only intention were to entertain you. Everything that happened in the previous chapters — every silence, every pause, every story, every biblical verse — had one purpose: to prepare you for this moment.

That sigh you just took... yes, that one... that is your spirit recognizing that this chapter is not theoretical. It is personal. God has not been training you to observe. He has been preparing you to respond. He does not waste words. *"He who has ears to hear, let him hear"* (Matthew 11:15). And if you have heard His questions throughout this book, then you have been a candidate for His calling.

The Bible is full of people who thought they were only observing. Moses was tending sheep when he encountered the burning bush *(Exodus 3:1–4)*. Elijah was lamenting under a broom tree when God whispered a new destiny to him *(1 Kings 19:4–8)*. Martha was busy with dishes and tasks, never imagining that that moment in her home would be remembered for generations *(Luke 10:38–42)*. Bartimaeus went to sit, as always, by the roadside… and that day he ended up following Jesus on the road *(Mark 10:46–52)*.

> *God does not call spectators. He calls participants. And now He is calling you.*

YOUR STORY IS NOT AN OBSTACLE: IT IS RAW MATERIAL FOR THE CALLING

There was a season when I complained to God about my own failures. "Lord, if You knew my weaknesses, why did You call me? If You saw my wounds, why did You insist?" It felt unfair that He would ask me to serve Him when my scars were screaming so loudly. But His answer was not audible — and yet it was so clear that it made me stop in my tracks:

"Because your wounds do not disqualify My calling; they are the room where I will reveal Myself."

That is when I understood something I once heard preached in a single sentence and that God later confirmed in my own flesh: what you call a glitch, I call a bridge. A glitch is that failure, that system error that makes you want to throw away your phone, tablet, or computer because "it no longer works." But sometimes, with the right update, that same device ends up working better than before.

Your limitations, your failures, your "system errors" are not trash to God; they are the material He uses to build something that cannot be torn down. God has never used flawless lives. He uses available lives. God did not look for perfect speakers; He looked for Isaiah, willing to say, "Send me," on the day he heard the voice of the Lord say:

> *"Whom shall I send, and who will go for Us?"*
> *Then I said, "Here am I! Send me".*

(Isaiah 6:8)

HE DID NOT LOOK ONLY FOR BRILLIANT MINDS; HE LOOKED FOR CONTRITE HEARTS.

Scripture is a parade of people with far-from-impressive résumés:

- **Abraham** lied out of fear and yet was called the father of faith (Genesis 12:10–20).

- **Joseph** was sold, betrayed, and imprisoned before seeing his purpose fulfilled (Genesis 37; 39–41).

- **Moses** stuttered and carried the guilt of having killed an Egyptian (Exodus 4:10; 2:11–15).

- **David** was the youngest, ignored by his own father, and carried scars of sin and guilt (1 Samuel 16; 2 Samuel 11–12).

- **Peter** denied Jesus three times and yet was raised up to strengthen his brothers (Luke 22:54–62; John 21:15–19).

- **Martha** drowned in distractions until she learned that only one thing was necessary (Luke 10:38–42).

- **The woman with the issue of blood** carried twelve years of shame and rejection (Mark 5:25–34).

- **Bartimaeus** lived much of his life sitting on the margins of the road (Mark 10:46–52).

- **Saul** persecuted the church before becoming Paul, an apostle of Jesus Christ (Acts 9; Galatians 1:13–16).

And yet, God called them and used them.

The forcefulness of 1 Corinthians is unmistakable:

"But God has chosen the foolish things of the world to put to shame the wise, and God has chosen the weak things of the world to put to shame the things which are mighty; and the base things of the world and the things which are despised God has chosen, and the things which are not, to bring to nothing the things that are, that no flesh should glory in His presence."

(1 Corinthians 1:27–29)

What we see as a flaw, God sees as a canvas.

That means my *glitches* are not excuses to stay on the sidelines; they are the canvas on which God wants to display His grace. Stop thinking that your story is an obstacle. It is your seed. God saw you in your childhood, in your darkness, in every defeat. And as He said to Jeremiah:

"Before I formed you in the womb I knew you;
Before you were born I sanctified you;
I ordained you a prophet to the nations".

(Jeremiah 1:5)

He is not surprised by your wounds; He turns them into platforms.

The calling is activated by a single phrase:

"Here I am. Send me."

I did not say, "Here I am, when I finish this process." Nor, "Here I am, if You promise it won't hurt." Nor, "Here I am, if You guarantee results."

I simply said, **"Send me."** And I discovered that this word is a bridge. There are prayers that open windows. But "send me" opens roads.

Isaiah 6 tells the story of a throne, a temple filled with smoke and seraphim, the prophet seeing the glory of God, becoming aware of his sin, and receiving purification. Immediately afterward, God asks, *"Whom shall I send, and who will go for Us?"* And Isaiah responds with the phrase that has echoed through centuries: *"Here am I! Send me" (Isaiah 6:8).* His availability activated his destiny.

The story we have walked through in this book is filled with people who, one way or another, chose to take the first step.

There are phrases that change destinies. **"Here I am"** is one of them. Do not underestimate the power of simple availability. If you dare to say it sincerely, God will dare to show you what He prepared long ago.

YOU DON'T NEED MORE RESOURCES: YOU ALREADY HAVE WHAT IS ESSENTIAL

Another great lie that paralyzes us is the belief that in order to respond to the calling we must have everything figured out: the perfect equipment, enough money, followers, influence, a special title. But God is not waiting for that. He needs three things—and He has already placed them within your reach:

Your availability.

Your sincere "yes," even if you are afraid. God will not force you to serve Him. He respects your freedom, but He longs for your participation. A heart that surrenders before Him is the cry that makes Him turn His face and smile.

His Word.

The Bible is not an accessory; it is your compass. It renews your mind and reminds you who you are in Christ. The psalmist said it this way:

"Your word is a lamp to my feet and a light to my path".

(Psalm 119:105)

Paul expressed it to the Ephesians by reminding us that we are:

"For we are His workmanship, created in Christ Jesus for good works, which God prepared beforehand that we should walk in them".

(Ephesians 2:10)

Without the Word, we make noise. With the Word, we make history.

His Spirit.

We are not alone in this. Jesus promised another Helper to guide us into all truth *(John 14:16–17)*. The Holy Spirit brings to remembrance what Jesus has said, convicts us, empowers us, makes us weep and laugh, and moves us to do things we would never do on our own. He is the One who wakes us in the middle of the night to pray, who makes us tremble in the presence of sin, who gives us courage to speak when we would rather stay silent.

Availability to move.
The Word to guide you.
The Spirit to sustain you.

Everything else… comes along the way.
Do not despise the simple things.
Do not say "I don't have" when you have God.

IT'S TIME TO WAKE UP

Let me be very honest. Sometimes the most dangerous battle is not visible sin. It is spiritual drowsiness. That lukewarm state where you know God is pushing you, but you keep saying "later." That lethargy where you hear His voice, but you keep postponing your obedience. That sleep where you are alive, but not awake.

If this book has done anything in you —if something moved, if a question disturbed you, or if a phrase opened your eyes—

then understand this: this is God shaking your shoulder. Telling you, "It's time." He has already given us His thoughts, as the psalmist declared:

> "How precious also are Your thoughts to me, O God! How great is the sum of them! If I should count them, they would be more in number than the sand; When I awake, I am still with You".

> (Psalm 139:17–18)

They are not thoughts meant to put you to sleep; they are ideas meant to be lived.

Do you remember when Jesus was in the boat with the disciples and a storm broke out? He was sleeping, and they were panicking. They woke Him in fear: "Teacher, do You not care that we are perishing?" And Jesus arose, rebuked the wind and the sea, and said:

> "Peace, be still."
>
> "Then the wind ceased and there was a great calm. And He said to them, 'Why are you so fearful? How is it that you have no faith?'"

> (Mark 4:39–40)

It was not only a lesson about miracles; it was a confrontation of their mindset. They were physically awake, but spiritually asleep.

Sleeping in the middle of your calling is dangerous. You can lose unrepeatable moments. You can turn small disobediences into great storms. You can end up like Saul before Damascus: running fast, but in the wrong direction (Acts 9:1–2).

That is why, let me say it out loud:

Wake up!

Not strong. Not perfect. Just awake. Because when someone wakes up, everything changes. They see what they once ignored. They feel what they once numbed. They hear what they once silenced. And they respond to God with obedience where before they justified themselves, delayed, or hid.

BEFORE SENDING YOU, GOD WANTS TO MAKE SURE YOU ARE AWAKE

God is not looking for robots who obey without a heart. He is looking for sons and daughters who obey out of love. That is why, before sending you, He secures your awakening. You may feel weak, but the apostle declared:

> *"I beseech you therefore, brethren, by the mercies of God, that you present your bodies a living sacrifice, holy, acceptable to God, which is your reasonable service. And do not be conformed to this world, but be transformed by the renewing of your mind, that you may prove what is that good and acceptable and perfect will of God".*
>
> *(Romans 12:1-2)*

That is awakening. Presenting yourself. Renewing your mind. Breaking worldly molds and embracing the mind of Christ *(1 Corinthians 2:16).*

Spiritual awakening does not always come with thunder and lightning. Sometimes it looks like a sigh in the kitchen while you're washing dishes, when you sense God saying, "Why don't you start encouraging that neighbor you always see alone?" Sometimes it shows up while you're driving and suddenly decide to turn off the radio and pray out loud. Sometimes it's a text message to someone you need to forgive. Sometimes it's signing up for a Bible course. Sometimes it's volunteering to serve in your church, even if it's just to welcome people with a smile. Do not despise those awakenings. They are the prelude to your calling.

THE CALLING IS NOT FOR GIANTS: IT IS FOR REAL PEOPLE

I also used to believe that God only called the "great ones." The ones from the Bible. The ones on pulpits. The ones who never fail. But the Bible is not filled with giants. It is filled with ordinary people who were obedient in extraordinary moments. People who said "yes" when there was risk. People who let go of comfort to embrace the divine adventure.

The author of Hebrews wrote about them in what we now call the hall of faith—men and women who, by human standards, should never have made the list *(Hebrews 11)*. Among them were people with complicated stories, exiles, foreigners, men and women who endured as seeing "the Invisible."

They are there not because of their perfection, but because of their faith. And they all shared something in common: they obeyed what they understood and trusted what they did not.

God is not waiting for you to become a hero before He calls you. He calls you so that, in His hands, you may become a testimony of His greatness. So if you feel small, weak, or inadequate, you are in excellent company.

THE CALLING IS IN YOUR HANDS (LITERALLY)

As I write these final lines, I look at my own hands. They are not famous hands. They are not perfect hands. They are not theological hands. They are human hands—and yet, God chose to write His story upon them. And now I look at your hands. Perhaps shy. Perhaps trembling. Perhaps wounded. But ready.

Let me remind you of Psalm 139:

The calling is in your hands (literally)

"For You formed my inward parts; You covered me in my mother's womb. I will praise You, for I am fearfully and wonderfully made; Marvelous are Your works, And that my soul knows very well. My frame was not hidden from You, When I was made in secret, And skillfully wrought in the lowest parts of the earth. Your eyes saw my substance, being yet unformed. And in Your book they all were written, The days fashioned for me, When as yet there were none of them. How precious also are Your thoughts to me, O God! How great is the sum of them!"

(Psalms 139:13-17)

That means your hands were designed for something specific. They are not the product of chance. They are not an evolutionary accident. They are a divine masterpiece. In them, God will place tasks, seeds, and opportunities.

Every time you hold a phone to call someone who needs

hope, you are being called. Every time you embrace a child who is doubting, you are responding. Every time you write a message that inspires another, you are saying, "Here I am." Every time you hand a bag of food to someone who is hungry, you are living out your calling. Do not underestimate the ordinary. It is the stage of the eternal.

God does not place a book like this into hands that will not be used. If it is in your hands… it is because you are part of what God is doing.

THIS IS THE MOMENT YOU DECIDE

Not tomorrow. Not after you heal. Not when you finally feel "worthy." Today. Here. You and God. He asked. He interrupted. He spoke. He formed you. He prepared you. And now He looks at you—not to examine you, but to listen.

The Holy Spirit is a gentleman. He will not force you to rise, but He will invite you. The world wants many projects; God is looking for a heart. Culture celebrates plans; God embraces yeses. This chapter does not demand a schedule from you; it demands a posture—a posture of surrender, of yielding, of openness.

Imagine Isaiah breathing deeply in the temple as he hears the heavenly question. He could have said, "I'm busy with the sacrifices." He could have said, "Send the seraphim." He could have said, "Send me tomorrow." But he didn't. He answered from the depths of his being: "Here I am." And that echo is still resounding thousands of years later.

Today, your voice can join that echo. And perhaps, fifty years from now, someone will be inspired by your yes. Perhaps a child watching you serve will think, "If he could do it, so can

I." Perhaps your obedience will be the seed of a revival in your community. Perhaps your yes will be the whisper that awakens another sleeping soul.

HERE I AM

We have reached the final lines, and my heart is beating fast—not out of fear, but out of expectation. I feel as if I am writing these words in the company of angels who celebrate every decision made in secret. Because I know I am not writing for a passive reader. I am writing for someone who is about to answer God with everything.

Lord...

If this book has served any purpose, let it be this:
Here I am.

I do not have everything figured out. But I have **Your Word,** which reminds me that I am Your masterpiece, *"Your workmanship, created in Christ Jesus for good works"* (Ephesians 2:10).

I do not have all the answers. But I have **Your Spirit,** who intercedes for me with groanings too deep for words:

> *"Likewise the Spirit also helps us in our weaknesses. For we do not know what we should pray for as we ought, but the Spirit Himself makes intercession for us with groanings which cannot be uttered".*
>
> *(Romans 8:26)*

I do not have a complete map. But I have Your voice, which tells me:

"Your ears shall hear a word behind you, saying, 'This is the way, walk in it,' whenever you turn to the right hand or whenever you turn to the left".

(Isaiah 30:21)

And that is enough.

If You were waiting for me to wake up... I am awake now.
If You were waiting for my availability... here it is.

If You were waiting for my answer... I give it to You:
Send me.

Wherever You want. Whenever You want. However You want. I offer You my fear, my courage, my joy, and my sorrow. I give You my trembling hands and my uncertain voice. I give You my good days and my bad days. I give You my broken dreams and my most hidden longings. Use me. Transform me. Sustain me. Speak. Guide. Change me.

And when my voice trembles... You speak for me. And when my feet hesitate... You push me forward. And when obedience is hard... remind me of this moment. Not another day. Not another season. **Today.**

This is the chapter where I say "yes." And this "yes" will be the echo that follows me into everything that comes next—not because I am great, but because You are.

Here I am. Send me.

WILL THESE BONES LIVE?

THE LAST QUESTION GOD ASKS YOU BEFORE SENDING YOU

There are questions God asks while you are walking…

and there are questions He only asks when you can't go on any longer. That is why this book could not end on a mountain, nor with a glorious calling, nor on a spiritual platform.

It had to end in a valley: dry, silent, filled with bones where there is no appearance of life left.

Because before launching a man or a woman into their calling, God asks the question that exposes everything:

"Will these bones live?" (Ezekiel 37:3)

This is not a question for the strong. It is a question for the honest. For the one who knows there are areas inside that died long ago. For the one who wants to say "yes," but carries weariness, guilt, doubts, interruptions, and seasons where the soul dried up without realizing it.

THE VALLEY DOES NOT DENY YOUR CALLING; IT REVEALS WHERE YOU NEED THE SPIRIT

Ezekiel did not arrive at the valley by mistake. God led him there. This is what happens to the one who has said, "Lord, here I am": God shows you not only where He wants to use you, but which part of you needs resurrection first. Because there are callings spoken with courage, but sustained only by the Spirit. And in that valley God shows you: "No matter how well you speak, how much you know, or how hard you try. Without My breath... there is no life."

THE MOST HONEST ANSWER IS ALSO THE ONE THAT OPENS HEAVEN

When God asks, "Will these bones live?" Ezekiel does not respond with heroic faith or deep theology.

He simply says:

"O Lord God, You know". (Ezekiel 37:3)

That phrase is not defeat; it is surrender. It is admitting: "Lord, I can speak, but only You can breathe." "I can obey, but only You can bring life." This is the heart of true calling: a humble yes, not a perfect one.

THE CALLING GOD GAVE YOU DOES NOT DIE IN YOUR HANDS; IT LIVES IN HIS BREATH

Ezekiel spoke. The bones came together. The tendons appeared. Flesh covered the bodies. The structure was formed. But still, there was no life.

Because you can have order, discipline, devotion, Scripture, gifts, talents... and still be empty inside.

YOU OBEY... AND GOD BREATHES

Then God tells him: "Prophesy to the Spirit." And when the Spirit breathes, the valley changes. The bones rise. Hope returns. And what seemed impossible becomes an army.

This is the final message:
God did not call you because you are alive.
He called you because He intends to breathe.

YOUR VALLEY IS NOT YOUR END; IT IS YOUR EVIDENCE

That place where you yourself say:
"This will not live again."
"This cannot be fixed."
"This is already dead."

Right there God wants to display His glory.
Right there God wants to rewrite your story.
Right there God wants to show that the calling does not depend on your strength, but on His Spirit.

You are not called because you are strong,
nor because you are ready,
nor because you are in control.

You are called because God saw a valley in you
and decided to breathe.

CLOSING

Do not fear dry bones.
Do not fear silence.
Do not fear pauses.
Do not fear places where you no longer see life.

Because if God asked you the question…
He also has the answer.

And when He breathes,
everything you thought was dead
will rise.

Acknowledgments

To my Lord Jesus,
who sought me when I was not seeking Him, who called me by name even when I was sincerely mistaken, and who turned my pauses into a path. Everything I am, everything I write, and everything I hope to become… flows from Your grace.

To Milka,
the companion God prepared for my heart. Thank you for your patience, your counsel, your wisdom, your discernment, your timely embrace, and for walking with me even through my most awkward processes. God used your voice to stop me when I did not know how to stop myself.

To my children, Christian, Joel, and Jonathan,
my inheritance, my legacy, and my greatest prayer.
You are the deepest questions God has asked me, and also the most unexpected answers.
This book was born thinking of you… and of the generation coming behind you.

To Mamita, Rosaura.
Thank you for being a firm pillar in my life, for your courage in moments where others would have fallen, for your silent yet powerful leadership, and for your example of faith, discipline, sacrifice, and love. You are a stronghold of a woman—unique, chosen by God to mark my story more than you can imagine. Many of the seeds of this book were first planted in your heart.

To my in-laws, Nicolás and Amparo.
Thank you for your example, your unshakable faith, your life surrendered to the Lord, and the footprints you have left in our family.
Amparo, thank you for agreeing to write the foreword of this book. Your words arrived at the right moment and reflect a heart sensitive to the voice of the Spirit. I honor your willingness and your obedience.

To Elizabeth Vargas, my editor.
Thank you for your dedication, your excellence, your detailed eye, your care for every word, and your passion for the work of the Lord. God used you not only to polish a manuscript, but to refine a mission. Your labor has eternal impact.

To my extended family,
to those who have been part of my story, my processes, my highs and lows. Every conversation, every prayer, and every embrace formed chapters within this chapter.

To the friends
who stayed close even when my paths were crooked—those who listened to my frustrations, celebrated my small steps forward, and corrected me with love.
You are part of the "Saul, Saul…" that led me back to Christ.

To my brothers and sisters in the faith,
to teachers, pastors, mentors, leaders, and ministry companions who in one way or another marked my steps. Many of you were "Ananias" sent by God when I least expected it.

To the readers.

Thank you for opening these pages with a willing heart.

I pray that every question in this book becomes an echo of the Spirit in your soul, and that you too discover that God does not call the perfect, but the available.

All the glory, always,
to the One who keeps asking:

"Is there anyone...?"

FOR THOSE WHO WISH TO KNOW WHERE THE JOURNEY BEGAN

Before **Is There Anyone?,**
this journey began with a first book:

Nicolas: The Legacy of a Man of God

A story of lived faith, quiet obedience,
and spiritual inheritance.

This book is not required to read the one
you hold in your hands, but it may help you understand
the origin of many of the questions, themes, and callings
that echo throughout these pages.

About the Author

Saul Miranda is a husband, father, leader, and writer who has learned to listen to God along the least expected paths. Born in Puerto Rico and established in Florida, Saul has devoted his life to serving with excellence both in his professional field and in his spiritual walk.

He began his professional formation in the field of communications, earning a bachelor's degree in Communications with a concentration in Advertising, as well as an associate degree in Graphic Arts. During that season, he worked in print media such as El Nuevo Día Orlando and La Prensa, developing a special sensitivity for storytelling, design, and the power of the written word. Those years laid the foundation for the way he communicates today: clearly, humanly, and with intention.

For nearly ten years, he worked in the luxury hospitality industry—at JW Marriott and Ritz-Carlton Orlando—where he began in entry-level positions and eventually became a bakery supervisor. Later, his journey led him to Disney, where he currently serves as an **Assistant Pastry Sous Chef at Magic Kingdom.** His leadership is marked by humility, creativity, empathy, and a deep desire to help others grow while he himself continues to be formed.

But beyond the culinary craft, Saul is a man marked by grace.

His story is filled with divine interruptions, unexpected pauses, deep processes, and moments when God asked him—like so many biblical characters—the questions that change a life. From those conversations with heaven, his books are born.

He is the founder of **Editorial Semillas de Luz,** a project that combines his passion for pastoral teaching, intimate writing, and the desire to leave a spiritual legacy for his children and future generations. His first book, Nicolás: The Legacy of a Man of God, honors the faith and testimony of his father-in-law, a faithful servant who marked his entire family. Is There Anyone? is his second work—a biblical and personal journey through the questions God asks when He wants to awaken a heart.

Saul writes the way he speaks: with honesty, humor, vulnerability, and a prophetic edge. His pages are filled with humanity, but also with hope. He does not aim to be an expert; he aims to be available. He does not write from perfection, but from the grace that reached him.

He lives in Davenport with his wife Milka—his companion, his best friend, and God's most precise gift—and their sons Christian, Joel, and Jonathan, who are his greatest inspiration and his most cherished ministry.

For Saul, every book is a seed.

Every chapter is a conversation.

And every divine question is an open door for others to discover that, even when we are sincerely mistaken...

God is still calling.

A RESPONSE IN WORSHIP

This book was born from a question.
The worship album Here I Am was born as the response.

Scan the code to continue
this calling through prayer and music.

www.ingramcontent.com/pod-product-compliance
Lightning Source LLC
Chambersburg PA
CBHW060409130626
46555CB00005B/2012